unf*ck your finances

MELISSA BROWNE

With thanks to Tony, the #baldsexyman, who cooks me soup, listens to me rant, knows I often take on too much and never says I told you so. It's official. Husband of the year.

WHEN I WAS LITTLE MY PARENTS WOULD WASH
MY MOUTH OUT WITH SOAP IF I SWORE. CAN
YOU IMAGINE WHAT THEY THINK OF THE TITLE
OF THIS BOOK?

BUT THE THING IS, IT'S NOT WRITTEN FOR THEM.
IT'S WRITTEN FOR YOU. THE GEN X/Y WHO SAW
THE TITLE AND CONNECTED WITH IT IMMEDIATELY.
I KNOW IF YOU READ IT, ABSORB IT AND DO
SOMETHING ABOUT IT, YOU CAN ACTUALLY DO IT.
UNF*CK YOUR FINANCES THAT IS.

THIS BOOK IS DEDICATED TO ANYONE WHO
FEELS LIKE THEY'RE SITTING AT THE BOTTOM OF
A DEEP HOLE, DESPERATELY LOOKING FOR THE
MAGIC DRINK OR MAGIC CAKE, UNSURE HOW THEY
ARRIVED THERE BUT ABSOLUTELY F*CKING SURE
THEY DON'T KNOW HOW TO GET OUT.

THIS IS THE LITTLE WHITE RABBIT.
FOLLOW ME.

ENJOY.
MEL X

unf*ck your finances

Perhaps our grandparents had it easier. There was a script, a financial path, an expected course to follow. They grew up, met a partner, married, bought a house, popped out a few kids, retired at 60, drew their pension, bought a caravan and looked after the grandkids during the holidays.

Today that script has changed.

House prices in many countries are skyrocketing, rents are galloping, technology is sprinting ahead and globalisation means our competitors and our next job could be anywhere.

Our households today are made up of the traditional family unit, singles, child-free couples, childless couples, gay couples, 'framilies' and more.

We have easy access to credit, the ability to spend 24/7, and a casual willingness to sacrifice our financial future for the right brand outfit bought online on credit to post on social media.

Many of us are more concerned with seizing the day and not worrying about tomorrow – because who knows what next week will bring, never mind next year or next decade. And retirement? It simply doesn't bear thinking about.

So, we don't.

I'm certainly part of this wave that is writing a new storyline. I've been married twice, lived in a house with six of my closest friends in my early thirties, have chosen with my now-husband not to have children, have co-founded three businesses, and spend my week split between a house in the mountains and an apartment in the city. I love the financial freedom of being able to design the life I want, but I also know I've had to work hard for this to become my reality.

That's because I've had to do a bloody good job of unf*cking my own finances. I've had to understand my compulsions, protect myself from self-sabotage and claw my way back from finding myself with less than nothing in my early thirties.

Now, I am fortunate in that I have a financially astute father who retired very well in his early fifties. I picked his brain during my financial black hole with all sorts of questions about investing, business, shares, property and more. Of course, I didn't tell him about my dire financial situation. I was far too ashamed – which, given we both have financial backgrounds, seems really silly now. But thankfully I at least had the sense to ask, listen and, most importantly, to act.

Most of us aren't lucky enough to have a dad whose financially savvy brain we can pick.

In fact, most of us weren't even taught the basics of managing our finances, whether by our parents at home, at school or at university. Sure, if we have a pile of cash we can talk to a financial advisor who will sell us a product or two – but what if we don't?

Which is exactly why I wrote this book.

Because if you're in a position where you know your finances need some unf*cking, or you suspect you're on a slippery slope to your own financial black hole, then let this book be the little savvy brain you can pick. One that starts you on your own path to financial wholeness.

Now, needing to unf*ck your finances doesn't necessarily mean you have a whole lot of debt. Although for some of you that's exactly what it does mean. Instead, it can mean helping you learn how to financially grow up.

To financially adult.

Unf*cking your finances can mean understanding how to get into a habit of saving rather than spending, figuring out how to set up your bank accounts, tricks to help you save money without you even realising it, investments you should know about, why you shouldn't budget, and how to become not just financially unf*cked, but financially well.

The first step to financial wellness is to unf*ck your finances.

For some of you there's just no way around it. You need to seriously sort yourself out. Financially, that is. To start to dig yourself out of the hole you've created, or to jump on the brakes before you end up too much further down the hill. You need to work out what you're doing, why you're doing it and figure out a new way of doing things that works for you.

The second step is to create financial resilience.

This means starting to show some financial grit, building up financial toughness and beginning to feel financially strong. You might have paid down your debt, built up some savings, gained an understanding of where your money is going, started investing, and now you're beginning to see some results.

Of course, we could just stop there. I mean, surely having financial resilience is a great thing?

Perhaps. But personally, I don't ever want resilience to be my end game.

That's because I see resilience as a gritty thing. It's a teeth-clenched, finger-tip-gripping, pushing-through-to-the-end kind of state. And it's what many of us aspire to. It's what we want for our lives, our finances, our children. The ability to bounce back. To be resilient.

After all, isn't that what unf*cking your finances means? To become financially resilient?

Not quite.

Sure, I'm incredibly happy to have the qualities of resilience – but I don't want simply to be recovering from aftershocks in life. Instead, I think resilience needs to be something we pass through or perhaps have in our toolkit on our way to the end game of financial wellness.

Which is why the third step is to become financially well.

Not to simply suffer our financial situation, or wait for Prince Charming, a fairy godmother or a lottery ticket to come and rescue us, but to grab those glass slippers and rescue ourselves.

At the end of the day unf*cking your finances, developing financial resilience and, ultimately, embracing financial wellness starts with you. And hopefully begins with the book that's in your hands now.

So, take a deep breath, pour yourself a glass of wine if need be, and let's begin your next financial chapter.

"OUR CULTURE TEACHES US ABOUT SHAME
– IT DICTATES WHAT IS ACCEPTABLE AND
WHAT IS NOT. WE WEREN'T BORN CRAVING
PERFECT BODIES. WE WEREN'T BORN
AFRAID TO TELL OUR STORIES. WE WEREN'T
BORN WITH A FEAR OF GETTING TOO OLD
TO FEEL VALUABLE. WE WEREN'T BORN
WITH A POTTERY BARN CATALOGUE IN ONE
HAND AND HEART-BREAKING DEBT IN THE
OTHER. SHAME COMES FROM OUTSIDE OF US
– FROM THE MESSAGES AND EXPECTATIONS
OF OUR CULTURE. WHAT COMES FROM THE
INSIDE OF US IS A VERY HUMAN NEED TO
BELONG, TO RELATE." BRENÉ BROWN

why are we so financially f*cked up?

You can't write a book with f*ck in the title and not talk about sex. It's simply necessary.

Let's start our sex chat with the ultimate bad sex guide, *Fifty Shades of Grey*. Why start here? Because I was asked to speak at the launch of the movie in Melbourne. Now, I appreciate it may seem strange to ask a financial advisor to speak about money before a film that is almost completely about sex. Perhaps you're thinking I was the metaphorical bucket of cold water.

Whatever the reason, I was so glad to be asked.

Not because I wanted to watch *Fifty Shades of Grey*. I still haven't read the book and wouldn't have watched the movie if left to my own devices. Not because I'm a prude. I simply object to bad storylines. After all, if I'm going to fill a sneaky few hours with sex, I'd rather fill them with sex and fashion by watching an episode of *Sex and the City*, or sex and laughter by listening to a podcast of *My Dad Wrote a Porno*. Sex and awkwardness while sitting in a dark theatre with fifty others, watching Christian Grey earnestly spank someone, just doesn't appeal to me. Strangely.

So why was I so happy to speak before a movie I felt so uncomfortable about?

Because of the connection between sex and money.

Once upon a time sex had an almighty 'ick' factor associated with it. Sex simply wasn't a subject that was talked about in polite company. Nice girls didn't talk about it – and they certainly didn't own up to wanting more of it or, even more scandalous, enjoying it!

Thanks to *Sex and the City* and other television series, books, magazines and movies that dealt with it irreverently and cleverly, it gradually became OK to talk about sex. Not just over cocktails (when you hoped you wouldn't remember the conversation in the morning) – suddenly it's OK to talk blowjobs over brunch.

Somehow the ick factor was removed from sex because the shame was lifted. Simply by bringing the subject into the light of day and talking (and laughing) about it.

Fast forward to me, an accountant and money expert, talking financial fairy tales to a bunch of women (and some poor blokes) who had flocked to watch a movie that was unashamedly about sex.

I, for one, would love money to be given the same treatment.

Now, some might argue it already has. The movie *The Wolf of Wall Street* certainly idolised money, and there have been many books and films both before and since in which the making of money has been lauded.

But what about the vulnerability associated with money? What about the shame?

What about the ick factor, which means we aren't prepared to have those awkward money conversations (which is most money conversations that don't involve property prices if we're completely honest)? So we don't ask a girlfriend during a long lunch if she's racking up a large credit card bill because she seems to be doing a little too much emotional spending. We don't want to cause offence by asking a beloved relative whose husband has passed away if she is going to be able to pay the bills. And we don't talk about exactly how much we want our business to net in profit, because we don't want to be judged.

I've found myself in all three financial scenarios and I'm sure you can relate to at least one of them. The question I have for you is, did you speak up? If not, why?

I can answer that for you. It's the reason why for at least one of those situations I said nothing. We still feel awkward, uncomfortable and impolite talking about money.

Which is exactly why we need to start having real conversations about finances.

A couple of years ago, I met with a good friend to talk about her business. I think she beautifully described why we don't talk about money. At our very first meeting it quickly became clear she felt she wasn't in a great place financially and was very embarrassed about it. She told me she felt incredibly vulnerable about coming to see me – and gave me a long explanation as to why that was, before she even began to talk about finances. She even told me that she'd cancelled the appointment twice and had been tempted to cancel again. Eventually, just as I thought we were finally able to get started, she stopped, grabbed my arm and said, 'I feel like I'm about to get naked.'

Her choice of words and her vulnerability capture why I was so pleased to be invited to speak before a movie that was all about sex.

The reason so many women leave the lights off in the bedroom when having sex is the same reason we're also leaving the lights off on our finances. We're ashamed that someone will see and judge us.

And, often, even we ourselves don't want to acknowledge the mess we're in. Which means, yes, I know some of you aren't even opening bank statements or other financial correspondence you don't feel comfortable with!

If you can't look at something or talk about something, it's going to have an almighty ick factor attached to it. Which is exactly what's happening with money.

Part of the reason I believe we're so vulnerable and feel so icky about money is because of the extremes associated with it.

If you don't have enough money, if you're not earning what you think you should be, or if you have too much debt, there can be enormous shame involved. Perhaps it's because we worry what people will think of us if they see the financial mess we're in. Or perhaps we don't think we're earning enough to keep up appearances for the suburb we live in, the school our kids go to, or the people we associate with. Whatever the reason, we're ashamed because of our perceived deficit.

Or perhaps it's more to do with the opposite extreme.

While it seems to be quite acceptable for men to say they want more money, is it OK for a woman to say she wants to be financially successful and wealthy? Particularly if, say, like me, she has chosen not to have a family? Or if she is a working mother? Does that make women selfish somehow, or less feminine? Is there judgement involved with women wanting to have more money, in the same way that, pre-Samantha, women might have felt embarrassed about coming out and saying they enjoyed sex and wanted more of it?

Or if you're a man and your wife is earning more than you, does that make you feel less of a man? Or only if your mates find out? What if you choose to stay at home and look after the kids for a year? Do the (mainly) women at the school gate think less of you because you're not a provider?

At the end of the day one thing is clear – even if we're not talking about money, there's a whole lot of judgement involved.

Which is why we may as well talk about it.

I believe we need to acknowledge the vulnerability and awkwardness involved with talking about money and have the conversation anyway. To begin talking about all facets of money, not just the socially acceptable parts like buying property – and, by talking about it, remove the ickiness.

So rather than talking over coffee or cocktails about your latest sexual adventures, why not move on to talking about money: your goals, your dreams, how you're going with them and where you're really at. It's time to turn on the light in the bedroom and also remove the ick factor from one of the last remaining taboos: money.

Or at the very least, get financially naked and take a good look at yourself in the mirror. Acknowledge your situation today for what it is. Perhaps it's not something you're proud of – but is it something you're prepared to work on?

I mean, for f*ck's sake, let's just get over ourselves and start adulting when it comes to money.

"You can have it all.
Just not all at once."
Oprah Winfrey

> "LIFE SHRINKS OR EXPANDS IN PROPORTION TO ONE'S COURAGE." **ANAÏS NIN**

let's get naked about money

I am not a naked person. I have never been comfortable with my own nakedness and I am completely uncomfortable with other people seeing me naked.

My husband, on the other hand, IS a naked person. He has no problem whatsoever with getting his kit off, regardless of who is around.

On top of not being a naked person I'm also not an over-sharer or a hugger. And I'd rather you didn't over-share or hug too. Hot tip there in case we ever meet!

Which means I know what I'm asking when I'm telling you to be vulnerable and get naked about money.

Interestingly, when I asked random groups of people whether they'd rather be caught out naked or have their bank statements leaked online, more than 90 per cent admitted they would rather be caught naked. From the twenty-year-old right through to the eighty-year-old.

So either there are a lot of people like my husband who are happy to get naked or, as I suspect, we feel far more vulnerable sharing our finances than our bodies.

Which is saying something.

Perhaps that's because it has become acceptable to own our bodies. After all, there has been a big push for body acceptance on social media.

From Australian media commentator Mia Freeman sharing her feelings about her 'confronting stomach' in a positive and amusing way, through to internet sensation Taryn Brumfitt posting her 'before' and 'after' body online (when the 'after' was her post-baby shot and the 'before' was a body-building shot), to models occasionally (and sensationally) appearing with no airbrushing on magazine covers, and celebrities being published every day with 'real bodies', complete with cellulite. Perhaps as a result of all this we're becoming more comfortable in our own skins. We're aware we don't have to achieve or even seek perfection when it comes to our bodies.

We've worked out that if celebrities, who have far more time and cash than us, can't achieve perfection, then maybe we should just relax and accept ourselves?

So why do we have a different opinion when it comes to our finances?

I think it's because we're not sharing. We're not talking about it. We're not willing to get naked.

After all, when you're thirty-three, and you've been battling a decade-long eating disorder, you're already incredibly ashamed of what you perceive as a weakness. But when you've gathered the nerve to leave your husband because he has chosen not to give up alcohol, it takes courage. Particularly when you know friends won't understand and your religious parents may turn their backs on you. And financially you can barely support yourself. Your business can't sustain a regular wage because you've been trying to escape your life, so a mortgage is out of the question, which means moving into a shared house with six friends. And sure, donating the entire divorce settlement proceeds to charity seemed like a good idea at the time – a reaction to him saying you'd never make it on your own. But now you're wondering if that emotional reaction was a huge mistake. That's because, financially, you're f*cked. You're facing payroll next week, you have a stack of bills to pay and literally £100 in the bank. At this point everything feels overwhelming, but you're too embarrassed to tell anyone what is going on: both the reasons why you left and your dire financial situation. You're deeply ashamed of what you perceive as your failures.

Sexy, right? I mean, why wouldn't we want to share that stuff?

The truth is, if I'm honest, that's what I felt like at thirty-three. An accountant. Someone who was supposed to be able to talk about money. At an age when I was supposed to be starting to get my financial shit together. Surely it begs the question, how does someone who's not OK with money cope?

We cope, we become financially unstuck, financially un-f*cked if you will, by starting to share our stories.

Did I love sharing my story just now? Absolutely not! Did I rewrite it, take bits out, fret over it and delete it more than a few times? Absof*ckinglutely! Did I take a deep breath, put on my big-girl pants and decide to get naked anyway? Eventually.

Because what Mia Freeman is doing with her stomach, what Taryn Brumfitt did by posing naked, what the girls in *Sex and the City* did, what the editors at *Cosmopolitan* and a host of other magazines do regularly is dare to have real conversations about our bodies and about sex.

It's time we modelled the same vulnerability, the same nakedness, when it comes to money.

By sharing our secret money business we start to realise we're normal. By sharing our stories we can learn from each other's mistakes and build on them. By showing the highs and the lows we can encourage others to shoot for the stars and dig themselves out of the trenches.

That's because my story didn't end at financial devastation at age thirty-three. Instead, it morphed into a story of learning how to unf*ck my own finances, build resilience and, finally, build financial wellness – which is my (and I hope your) end goal.

How did I do that?

By figuring out how to build not just one business but three. By understanding how to invest in shares, in property, learning how to make great financial decisions that were right for me and, eventually, my husband, and determining what my financial DNA, values and priorities are.

It has meant ultimately designing a life I love and working out the finances I need to support it.

If I'm willing to share all parts of my financial story, if I'm willing to share the extreme highs and the extreme lows, and if I'm willing to be vulnerable, it means others can avoid the mistakes I've made and learn from what I did.

But it all starts with us getting naked.

Telling your money stories is something you can choose to do with your family, your friends, your kids and others. It's about starting real conversations about money.

How do you start?

It might be by inviting your girlfriend over for cocktails and telling her you want to talk about your financial aspirations, your goals and your secret money business (those things you're doing that you're not telling anyone about because you're kind of ashamed). It might be having a chat at the pub with a great mate who you think might be getting themselves into financial trouble. It might be inviting someone you suspect has great financial DNA out for lunch and picking their brain. It might be having an awkward conversation with a family member you think may be financially struggling. Or it might be confessing to a close girlfriend over brunch that it's you who is financially struggling – which you know she'll be horrified to learn because you're struggling to keep up.

The most important thing is to start.

Will it be awkward? Absof*ckinglutely. Will it occasionally not be received well? Undoubtedly. Will it ultimately be worth it because it will take some of your relationships to a deeper level and mean you're all working towards a common goal of financial wellness? In time, definitely.

Of course, if you need support then join me online and practise sharing using #secretmoneybusiness, or share your financial goals using #finspo.

While you're there take a look at what others have shared. Because sometimes it's empowering to realise so many of our money issues are so very common. Which means you're not alone and there are many others to learn from.

But it starts with you making the brave decision to be vulnerable about money. Join me and start embracing your financial nakedness.

"To love at all is to be vulnerable. Love anything and your heart will be wrung and possibly broken. If you want to make sure of keeping it intact you must give it to no one, not even an animal. Wrap it carefully round with hobbies and little luxuries; avoid all entanglements. Lock it up safe in the casket or coffin of your selfishness. But in that casket, safe, dark, motionless, airless, it will change. It will not be broken; it will become unbreakable, impenetrable, irredeemable. To love is to be vulnerable." CS Lewis

how to
break
up with
money

"A WISE PERSON SHOULD HAVE
MONEY IN THEIR HEAD, BUT NOT IN
THEIR HEART." JONATHAN SWIFT

how to break up with money

W hat is abundantly clear to me is that not only do we feel uncomfortable talking about money – and even thinking about money – but many of us don't have a great relationship with money. I mean, it's difficult to have a relationship with someone that you're not willing to talk to or think about.

Which is why for many of us our so-called relationship with money has turned toxic.

Let's be honest, if money was a bad boyfriend (or girlfriend) we would quickly kick it to the kerb!

The problem is that, unlike an inconsiderate partner, money is something we're stuck with. But unlike a normal relationship, we can dictate terms. Which is why, instead of working on our relationship with money, I believe many of us need to start by taking a break from it.

An 'it's not you, it's me' type trial separation.

Now, I appreciate that this is easier said than done. After all, if we compare money to another of our daily requirements – food – we can see another, often toxic, relationship.

Many of us spend a lot of our time thinking about food: what we're going to eat, when we're going to eat it, and whether we can start eating now. And in most Western countries this has resulted in larger and larger waistlines. Or we spend our time trying not to think about food. Which means food can be just as big a problem for the intentionally underweight as the overweight.

We reward ourselves with food when we're good. We deny ourselves when we're bad. We're constantly trying to break up with it. Yet, if we're honest, we behave like little children let loose in the snack cupboard most of the time.

Little wonder we don't have a great relationship with food.

Yet there is a movement to rein it in. To break up with the food we've been eating. To forge a new relationship with real food that is actually good for us.

Among others, people like Jamie Oliver and his Ministry of Food, Hugh Fearnley-Whittingstall, and Deliciously Ella talk about getting back to basics when it comes to food – and many of us have listened. We're mindful about where our food has come from, we want to know how the animals we eat have been treated, we're conscious of what we put into our bodies, and we're careful to eat food that is free from chemicals, preservatives and other nasties.

It's time we broke up with money too.

That's because we need to stop how we're currently behaving and begin a new relationship with money.

One we're not ashamed of. One we're not tempted to leave at home in a cupboard and hope it won't escape and embarrass us.

How we do that, how we begin anew, is also how we begin to unf*ck our finances.

That's because the unf*cking means stopping. That's why there's a big 'UN' in front of it. If we want to unf*ck our finances we need to break up with money and begin a new, healthy relationship that we're not just unashamed of but kind of proud of as well.

I CAN'T PROMISE BREAKING UP WITH MONEY WILL
BE EASY, BUT HERE ARE MY TOP TEN TIPS TO HELP
YOU THROUGH IT. AS YOU WORK THROUGH THIS
BOOK, WE'LL LOOK AT MOST OF THESE TEN STEPS
(AND MORE) IN A WHOLE LOT MORE DETAIL. THIS
IS JUST A LITTLE TEASER TO HELP EASE YOU GENTLY
INTO THE CONCEPTS.

1 **Do a financial detox.** If you're going to break up with
someone you need space and time apart. You need to
unfollow them on social media and start to separate your life
from theirs. It's no different with money. In order to break up
with money I recommend you begin with a financial detox.
This will enable you to realise how you act with money and
press 'reset'. A detox isn't anything fancy or spiritual. It's
simply thirty days of buying nothing new or non-essential.
And no, shoes are not essential.

2 **Understand how you think and feel.** You may have
heard about emotional eating – well, emotional spending
is just as bad for your health. Thoughts like, 'It's been a tough
month, I deserve something pretty'; or 'I work hard, I deserve
a £50,000 car'; or 'My child won't succeed without us spending £20,000 per year on schooling' aren't helpful for you,
your family or your wallet. It's also important to understand
how you think about money. Perhaps you've been brought up
to believe 'a man always takes care of a woman financially',
'people with too much money are selfish', or 'money is the
root of all evil'. If you don't understand how you think about
money you could be unconsciously sabotaging your relation-

ship with it. It's about taking the time now to become aware of the money messages you've either subconsciously or consciously received and are carrying around with you.

3 **Understand your values.** If you want to transfer your feelings from money onto something more worthwhile, make a list of what you value in life. Maybe it's freedom, family, security, influence or loyalty. Once you've worked out what your values are you're going to take a look at your goals and decide whether they fit with your values. Sometimes we just parrot goals because they're ones we think we should have. So 'I want to own my own home' is many people's goal – but is it really true for you? Or is it just what you think you should want? If one of your values is the freedom to chase your dream job around the globe, then sure you may want to own property (such as an investment property), but owning your own home might not be right for you now.

4 **Work out your goals.** At some point, a couple will work out together where their relationship is heading. If you want to start thinking about what your new relationship with money might look like, then it's important to work out what your goals are in life. I appreciate it's tough to look too far ahead but I believe twelve-month and three-year goals are essential. Together we're going to look at the best way to do this and, most importantly, we're going to make sure they're goals you're actually excited about.

5 **Work out a plan.** Sometimes goals and values can seem so far removed from your current situation that it's easier to just buy a cocktail and continue as you are. Maybe go ahead and order the cocktail – but once you do we're going to work out how much money it will take to effect the plan you've set, and how long it will take to action it. So, if your goal means you need £5,000 in twelve months' time, that means you need to save £100 per week. In this step we're going to turn money into something a little bit sexy and, perhaps, even something you might want to bring out on a date once in a while. Plans based on goals and values are attractive to us because they're meaningful. We're also going to look at different ways you can save money and different ways to invest your money. That's because you may have a goal but absolutely no idea of the best way to get there. Which is where planning and strategy kicks in.

6 **Understand how you're spending.** If you're in a bad relationship you need to face up to exactly what's going on and why it's not working. It's the same with money. After your financial detox it's time to understand where your money is going by tracking your spending using one of the many Cloud-based solutions available. This means you can start to recognise the behaviours and decisions that have f*cked up your current relationship with money so you can do something about them with your new relationship. I've listed a whole bunch of these apps at the end of the book. Now, before you start to itch, I didn't mention the B word. I'm not talking about a budget here. Instead, it's about becoming aware of how you're spending your money and knowing exactly where it's going.

7 Start to become a conscious consumer. Working out a plan is great, but unless you're monitoring it regularly it's too easy to go off track. Together we're going to work out a time (potentially every month) to check how you're going, see if you're on track and make any necessary adjustments. After all, it's far easier to lose a kilo as soon as it sneaks on than to get rid of 20kg accumulated over time. By jumping on the scale with your money regularly you'll be able to keep your eye on it and make adjustments before you feel as though it's a lost cause.

8 Remove yourself from temptation. I don't have any chocolate in the house because I have absolutely no willpower. Sure, I could decide I want to get tougher and purposely keep it in the house, but I'd be beating myself up daily because I know I'd eat it. It's the same with money. If you know you never window-shop but always window-buy, then don't window-shop. If you know that brunch with girlfriends always ends up as a Saturday afternoon shopping trip, suggest to them that you move brunch to a retail-free location instead. In this step we're going to look at removing temptation now that you know what you want, rather than continually waving a big stick at yourself.

9 Seek help from a relationship counsellor (aka money expert). Sometimes relationships just end up toxic and messy and we can't extract ourselves. It can be the same with money. You might have a go at all of the above and it just doesn't work for you – or you might know yourself well enough to know you need help from the start. We'll work out who you can talk to, what makes a great financial advisor and what they should offer to help you break up with money. It's also figuring out who are the best people in your life to recruit as your potential money mentors, cheerleaders, supporters and coach to make the going easier.

10 **Consistently monitor, gauge, adjust and track.** Establishing a healthy respect for money is a great thing to do. But just doing it once, giving yourself a big pat on the back and then getting back into the same old habits won't get you anywhere. So that you don't end up back in the same place you started (or worse), we're going to figure out how to make this a lifetime quest to not only keep your money under control, but also create an amazing relationship with it so that it gives you more freedom, empowerment and options. Three things I know most people want more of.

Of course, it's easy to list the 'ten steps to breaking up with money', but much harder to actually do them.

That's what the following chapters are all about. The how-tos. Along with a whole stack more to help you not just unf*ck your finances, but to understand them, trust yourself and gradually build your finances to a point where they help you create the life you want.

"You have to kick people out of your head as forcefully as you'd kick someone out of your house."
Sophia Amoruso, #GIRLBOSS

"THERE ARE 3 WAYS TO IMPROVE YOUR LIFE:
DO MORE OF WHAT'S WORKING, STOP DOING
WHAT ISN'T WORKING, AND TRY NEW THINGS
TO SEE WHAT DOES WORK." JACK CANFIELD

30-day financial detox

Most people who know me quickly appreciate that I love chocolate. By now we have an element of trust involved, so I'm just going to come out and say that I'm a chocolate addict.

Now, I know many people will say they have a chocolate addiction, but let me assure you that for me it's true.

I'm talking, can't have it in the house or on my person at all because it won't survive the day. OK, that's not entirely true. It won't survive the next few hours. OK, the next hour. I'm not talking a small chocolate bar either; I'm talking any quantity of chocolate whether it's a small, medium, large or family-size block. Which is why I try to limit my addiction to dark chocolate – selected brands only. To limit the damage to my waistline.

Like I said, I'm a chocolate addict.

From time to time I decide to give my body a break from my daily chocolate hit and eliminate all sugar for a month.

Initially my body hates me.

By the time I get to day five I am a walking, cranky headache and I'm sure my husband is working longer hours to avoid me. However, by the end of the month, if I'm honest, I would have to say I really don't miss my daily fix. Of course, what happens is that at the end of the month I reward myself with a piece of chocolate and the spiral takes about another six months before I feel the need to cleanse again.

What I realised very early on is that it can be the same with my finances. (Which, as you'll discover, is a running theme throughout this book.)

While I budget for the big purchases, I find it is the myriad smaller purchases made over time that hurt my bank account or credit card. Or the Christmas present/lunch/cocktails/drinks/event spending that merges into the Christmas and January sales until, in the end, I'm just handing over my credit card without registering what it's really costing me.

My solution to break the habit of this almost unconscious spending is the same as it is for chocolate. About twice a year, I decide to go for a month without buying anything new.

Now this might seem revolutionary, but it is enlightening to discover how much we unconsciously spend. Or how much we base our social and leisure time around buying stuff we don't need.

It might be a coffee with girlfriends and a window-shop, or a Wednesday night bored on the couch, online shopping with a bottle of wine. It might be scrolling through Instagram and clicking through to the brand's website to purchase, or perhaps it's impulse items at the supermarket.

It all just adds to the amount of stuff we accumulate and can, over time, put a sizeable dent in our bank account. As well as putting a dent in any financial goals we might have.

Which is why my solution to break this habit of spending is the same as for my chocolate addiction.

I cleanse my spending by choosing not to purchase anything new for thirty days.

Of course, groceries and other essential items aren't included in the financial cleanse, but everything else is off the table. No new clothes, shoes (the toughest one), make-up, books, stationery (another tough one) or any other 'stuff'. What it does is force me to become a conscious consumer for a month, breaking my habit of spending simply because I can.

It's up to you what is included in your 30-Day Financial Detox. If, like me, you spend your money on 'stuff', then make sure that anything tangible (other than groceries) is included in the detox. If you spend your money on entertainment, then make sure dinners out, alcohol and anything entertainment-related is included. The detox should be personalised to your own unique spending DNA.

And don't cheat.

Because sure, you might decide you can't bear not going out every Friday night and dropping £100 – but what if you didn't do it for a month? What unconscious behaviours might that reset? Never mind the cash you'll instantly save!

The 30-Day Financial Detox is something we recommend to everyone who undergoes coaching with our Mini Barre programme at my financial planning business, The Money Barre. As we're essentially working together, it's my recommendation for you too.

It's as easy as deciding not to consume anything new for thirty days.

If you decide to commit to a financial detox, I strongly encourage you to include your partner, friends, family and kids and educate them on why you're doing it. This means you'll not only be setting up great habits for all of you, but together you'll be creating a community of conscious consumers.

Besides, if your nearest and dearest are all doing this it's going to make it a whole lot easier for you!

Perhaps you could set aside some time each week where you talk about what you've learned about your spending habits, and how you might change how you do things together when the detox is over. It's a way of creating a financial language, making it OK to talk about money in a safe way and putting you all on an equal footing where you're financially supporting and encouraging one another.

IF THE IDEA OF DETOXING MAKES YOU BREAK OUT IN A SWEAT, OR YOU'RE WORRIED YOU'LL BE SITTING AT HOME KNITTING FOR THE NEXT THIRTY DAYS (ACTUALLY YOU CAN'T EVEN DO THAT BECAUSE IT WOULD MEAN YOU'D HAVE TO SPEND MONEY ON WOOL AND KNITTING NEEDLES!), HERE'S A BUNCH OF THRIFTY IDEAS THAT WILL HELP YOU STOP REACHING FOR YOUR WALLET.

✱ Head down to your local library and borrow a book instead of buying one.

✱ Fill the time you would spend shopping by volunteering at a local charity. You'll save money and feel good about yourself while doing it.

✱ Spend an afternoon decluttering your wardrobe, your kids' toys and your shed and sell what you don't need. Consider saving at least half the cash and donating the rest to charity.

✱ Work out your meals for the week, write a list of what you need, and then only buy what is on the list. If you know you'll be tempted to buy more, hand the list to someone you trust, along with your credit card, and ask them to buy everything online.

✳ Take advantage of free local events where you can be entertained and potentially fed and watered for nothing. Check out local guides for what's on near you.

✳ Become involved in market research and be paid in cash, or receive experiences or goods for your time.

✳ Go to the beach, go for a country walk or do something else active outdoors that is free but also makes you feel good.

✳ Take your credit and debit cards out of your wallet and only take the cash with you that you need.

✳ Look on the internet for retro games and spend an afternoon playing hopscotch, French skipping and basketball.

✳ Start a blog, diary or book. There's a story in everyone. If you still have grandparents, spend the afternoon with them and a video camera (or your phone) to record their stories.

If you're looking for more ideas check online and search for free things to do at weekends in your area.

The only thing left to for you to do is start. That's as easy as picking a date and simply doing it.

It's thirty days that will help you reset your spending and start you thinking differently (and consciously) about your finances. What do you have to lose?

"People say that money is not the key to happiness, but I always figured if you have enough money, you can have a key made." Joan Rivers

"ADVERTISERS HAVE US CHASING CARS AND CLOTHES, WORKING JOBS WE HATE SO WE CAN BUY SHIT WE DON'T NEED. WE'RE THE MIDDLE CHILDREN OF HISTORY, MAN. NO PURPOSE, NO PLACE."
TYLER DURDEN, FIGHT CLUB MOVIE

money mindful- ness

You've decided to do the 30-Day Financial Detox (good job, you), which means it's the perfect time to start working on becoming mindful around money. Something I suspect you've been actively avoiding up to now. Me? I struggle with being mindful.

I'm the person who watches TV, phone in one hand as I scroll through social media or tweet along with the show, balancing my laptop on my lap and replying to emails while trying not to spill my coffee and thinking about what I'm doing tomorrow.

I receive at least three hundred emails a day – never mind the Facebook, LinkedIn, Twitter and Instagram messages. All of which I try and respond to within twenty-four hours, as well as getting everything else done that I want to achieve. I run three businesses, have written three books in that time, write for multiple publications, speak at events and run workshops, all the while trying to be a great wife and good friend.

I get that it's f*cking tough to be mindful.

Which is why I understand that you may have rolled your eyes and sighed when you saw the word.

Yet, truth be told, in our fast-paced world it's exactly what we need to be.

Analysts tell us we've gone from being exposed to about 500 ads a day back in the 1970s to . . . well, experts simply can't agree on the number of messages we're now trying to absorb daily. Guesses range from 5,000 through to 20,000. What they do agree on is that our senses are being bombarded with over 11 million bits of data every second. The average person's working memory can handle 40–50 bits. That's it. Which means we ignore 10,999,950 bits of data every second we're awake.

If you feel like you're suffering from information overload just reading this, let me put it another way.

A study in 2011 showed that even back then the average person was bombarded by the equivalent of 174 newspapers a day – and we know that's increased. We also produced six newspapers' worth of information in 2011 compared with just two-and-a-half pages twenty-four years earlier. That's a 200-fold increase in information.

So, if you're finding the whole concept of mindfulness laughable perhaps that's because you can't imagine being able to do that. Be mindful, that is.

Yet when it comes to unf*cking our finances, that's exactly where we need to start.

While some of us are still cynics, more and more people are accepting that mindfulness is simply necessary. The health and wellness industry in particular has seen a boost in women becoming more mindful around their wellbeing. We're mindful as we pick out our co-ordinated lulu-lemon active wear; we're mindful as we're drinking our green smoothie with activated kale; and we're mindful as we're trying not to think about doughnuts when we're in the downward-dog position.

But I believe we're far less mindful when it comes to our financial health.

I mean, let's get real here.

In order to practise financial mindfulness you need to be willing to put financial thoughts into your, well, mind.

Which is something many of us actively avoid doing.

What do I think being financially mindful looks like? It's understanding and choosing to be aware of what we truly think about money. How we react to it. How we respond to triggers and stimuli.

It's also recognising what triggers our emotional spending, knowing what companies our pension is invested in, and being aware of our money mindsets, values and goals. It's applying the same care and concentration to our finances as we do to our physical health and wellbeing. It's figuring out why some days are harder than others when it comes to not spending. It's choosing to lean into those feelings and ask ourselves what is making us feel that way, and why.

Again, you're probably either nodding or rolling your eyes.

Me? I'd be rolling my eyes.

Because I'm not great with feelings. Let's talk pragmatic, let's talk practical, let's talk strategy – but feelings? Kill me now.

But here's the secret. It would be so easy to simply give you a financial strategy. Which of course is what we'll be doing together throughout this book. But if we don't look at the reasons why you're acting as you are, if you're not willing to question how you think and why you're at the point where you need to unf*ck your finances, then chances are you'll end up here again.

Which means we need to start practising money mindfulness, or 'moneyfulness' if you like.

Where to start? I believe we need to start questioning how we think and feel.

That is why I want you to do two exercises with me. Doing these while you're undergoing the Financial Detox is perfect timing and will stop you heading to the shops!

MONEY MINDFULNESS EXERCISE ONE

Often, when I meet clients, it becomes apparent that they associate right, wrong, good, bad (and sometimes even evil) with how they view money.

Examples of this might be:

✻ I don't think it's OK to have too much money (bad).

✻ I don't think it's OK to have debt – or debt is wrong (bad).

✻ I think it's OK to enjoy today (OK).

✻ I think it's good to be tight around spending, so I'm being smart with money (good).

✻ I think it's good to own your own home (good).

✻ I think it's OK to have some money, but not too much (OK/bad).

✻ I judge people who have too much money because it's not a good thing to have too much of (bad).

What I'd love you to do is figure out how YOU view money. Take a piece of paper, divide it into thirds, write GOOD, BAD and OK at the top of each section and make a list of various money-related scenarios and what you think of them. Or you can head to themoneybarre.com.au and download this sheet and the rest of the exercises in this chapter from the Unf*ck Your Finances Blog.

MONEY MINDFULNESS EXERCISE TWO

Or perhaps it's easier to think of money as a person that you're in a relationship with. On the other side of your piece of paper describe the relationship you have with money, as if money was a real person. How do you feel about it? How do you speak about it? How do you treat it and, in turn, how does it treat you? Do you respect it? Is it a good relationship? Is it a toxic one?

Examples of this might be:

✱ It's an abusive relationship.

✱ We have nothing in common.

✱ It's like a judgemental relative.

✱ It's a passive-aggressive relationship.

✱ Maybe we're Facebook friends, but we definitely don't hang out in real life.

✱ I've probably blocked you online.

✱ It's a trusted friend who supports me.

✱ It's like an ex-lover I can't stop thinking about.

It might seem ridiculous, but a lot of what we're doing is moving from looking at the 'what' and the 'how' to looking at the 'why'. That's because the 'why' is incredibly powerful, as marketing guru Simon Sinek points out in his Ted Talk on how great leaders inspire action.

If we can figure out the why, then the how and the what become significantly easier. That's because you can start to realise why you act the way you do. You might recognise the voice and actions of parents, friends or significant others in what you've written. You might be surprised that you think the way you do.

Hopefully, you can start to see how the thinking you've unconsciously been doing about money has potentially meant you've been sabotaging your finances.

There is a meme of a dog lying down and the caption reads, 'I can't adult today. Please don't make me adult.' It's cute and funny, but if you're applying this meme consciously or unconsciously to your finances then you're doing yourself a huge disservice.

That is why I believe you need to choose to move aside the clutter and be purposeful about your interaction with money. Which starts with becoming money mindful.

"SECURITY IS MOSTLY A SUPERSTITION.
IT DOES NOT EXIST IN NATURE, NOR
DO THE CHILDREN OF MEN AS A WHOLE
EXPERIENCE IT. AVOIDING DANGER IS NO
SAFER IN THE LONG RUN THAN OUTRIGHT
EXPOSURE. LIFE IS EITHER A DARING
ADVENTURE, OR NOTHING." **HELEN KELLER**

what do you value?

H opefully you've started to realise there are some internal money messages you've been carrying around that might have pushed you to a place where now your finances need a little unf*cking. You might even be wondering how you've never realised this before.

That's OK. Actually, it's more than OK, it's great! It means you're already beginning to think differently about money.

Next we need to look at your money values. But before we do, let's start with one of my values when it comes to something non-financial. My exercise values.

The truth is, I hate exercising.

I love how I feel after it, but I hate the monotony of exercising regularly. Unfortunately, it's not something you can just cram in for a day once a month and then not have to worry about. Otherwise I would absolutely do that.

Now, my confession with this exercising whinge is that twenty metres from my back door is a fully equipped gym.

My husband is a physiotherapist and used to work with a football club, so we have a fully functioning gym in our yard. So, it's not as if I need to even hop into a car and drive somewhere to work out. All I need to do is open the back door and walk into the yard.

Yet I still struggle with it.

Because a deep part of me doesn't value exercising.

My confession – and something I'm not proud of – is that I had an eating disorder for a decade, from my early twenties. Thankfully it's not something I now carry with me, but the problem is that I understand I can control my weight and how I look with what I put in my mouth. Which for years was a problem, because it meant I simply didn't value exercising as I had something else that made me feel and look (in my twisted mind, anyway) good.

I've tried to cultivate the feel-good part of exercise and value it. That motivation comes and goes. However, my deeper motivation, something I really value, is my wardrobe.

Which is why today it's the only real motivation I have for working out.

I love clothes. I've spent a small fortune on them over the years so I'm determined to be able to wear all my clothes for a long time to come. Which, unfortunately, means I need to embrace exercise – or restrict my calories – and I've come to love chocolate, wine and food way too much for that. Dammit!

I also know the benefits of exercise making you feel better, keeping you stronger in your old age, making you feel more vibrant, blah blah blah. For me, at this stage in my life, it really has come down to an exercise in economics. Exercising means I can extend the life of my wardrobe for as long as I remain the size I am.

Which is why I now value exercising. Because I value the wardrobe I've cultivated over the last couple of decades.

Now this may seem shallow, ridiculous and stupid – but so what? I could make myself look far better and talk to you about how I now value the health benefits of exercise, but it's a lie. The truth is I value my wardrobe. I've come to love food too much to restrict my calorie intake unnecessarily and, as a result, I now value exercise.

We need to do the same exercise on values (pardon the pun) when it comes to our finances.

Because we understand that, just like exercising, looking after our finances is important. We understand the rationale of spending less than we earn. We acknowledge that we want to look after ourselves financially throughout our life.

But we clearly don't value these pragmatic things because we're not doing anything about them.

Which is why it's time to get real and figure out what you really value. What will inspire you to take action that benefits YOU. What will motivate you enough to change what you're currently doing and transform your thinking so you want to change.

It all starts with values.

Again, I want you to do some work here. To not just passively read but rather to start figuring out how you think, how you feel, what you value about money. And so much more by the time we're done!

Understanding your values is a two-part process. You can grab a sheet of paper or you can head to themoneybarre. com.au and download this sheet and the rest of the exercises in this chapter from the Unf*ck Your Finances Blog.

PART ONE IS ABOUT ACKNOWLEDGING THE MONEY VALUES YOU'RE CURRENTLY CARRYING.

If we take it back to my exercise values, it's clear that I was carrying around messages that said 'exercising is unimportant because I can control my body with what I put or don't put in my mouth'. Which means I didn't value exercising enough to ever stick with it.

Unconscious money values and money messages are no different. Hopefully you've completed the exercise from the previous chapter and you've already started recognising some of these. The thing is, you're already carrying them around and they're already sabotaging you financially, so you may as well acknowledge them, call them out and work out what you want them to be.

If you're rolling your eyes and tempted to skip to the next chapter – don't.

The reason this is critical to figure out as we unf*ck your finances is because our values are what are most important to us in life. Research tells us that our values determine for us what is right and wrong, and how we judge good or bad. Our values are what motivate us towards different things in our life, just as they motivate us away from different things.

Values govern all human behaviour.

Why is why when creating change, we cannot only make changes to our mindsets, strategies and goals. We also need to check that our core values support these changes, and that they support the long-term results these changes are creating in our life.

Which starts with acknowledging what our values are.

Here we're primarily looking at your values around money, wealth and wealth creation.

Discovering consciously what is motivating and driving your life may be a revelation for you, or it may be a conscious reminder of what is important to you. Through it our aim is to discover why you may have internal conflict and, most importantly, start to reveal why you are not getting the financial results you want.

As always, be totally honest. Otherwise, why bother? This exercise is for you, after all.

Don't record or change your values, emotions or beliefs to appear in a positive light. This won't be a truthful representation of what is occurring for you and may prevent you from creating long-term sustainable change.

Just like my exercise values, the reason we're doing this is to acknowledge what your money values are and then evaluate whether they're driving the results you want in your life. Or evaluating whether you're trying to dupe yourself by carrying money values you've borrowed or inherited from someone else that you don't actually hold true for you.

So, grab your paper (or download from online) and, at the top, write Wealth Creation Values. Next it's time to write what your Wealth Creation Values are.

Examples of other people's Wealth Creation Values are:
✱ That I have money in the bank for now, later and the future.
✱ That I am in control of financial decisions.
✱ If I have too much money people will think I'm greedy.
✱ That I have independence and security.
✱ I'm always happy to bet on me.
✱ That my children always feel safe and cared for.
✱ That I have a large disposable income.

* I don't honestly care about money and I think less of people who do.
* That I have control.
* That I can do what I want when I want.
* That I travel abroad every year with my family.
* That I own my own home.
* That I'm able to design the life I want.
* I value options and freedom. I don't want to be tied down and I need choice.
* That a man should always be able to support a woman financially.

Now it's your turn. Take some time and write down YOUR Wealth Creation Values.

PART TWO NOW THAT YOU'VE WRITTEN DOWN YOUR WEALTH CREATION VALUES, LOOK AT THEM WITH A CRITICAL EYE. ASK YOURSELF IF THERE ARE ANY YOU'VE WRITTEN BECAUSE YOU THINK YOU SHOULD HAVE THEM. IF THEY'RE NOT REALLY YOURS, CROSS THEM OUT.

Once you've ended up with your values, the questions to ask yourself as you look at them are:

* Are your financial values getting you what you want from life?
* Are there any conflicts within your values preventing you from gaining what you desire?
* Are there any 'away froms' in your values, creating what you do not want? For example, if one of your money values

is 'To Not Be Poor', your unconscious mind does not process negatives, therefore creating you to 'Be Poor'. Rewrite these negative values as positive values.

✳ Are there any values you've received from a parent, friend or relative that you suspect may be unhelpful and might be preventing you from achieving the goals you want?

As you look at these questions, highlight the values that are perhaps unhelpful and ask yourself why they're unhelpful and how you ended up with them. Ask yourself why you're carrying them. Ask yourself what it might mean for you if these were different.

Make sure you look at the values you've written with a critical eye. That's because the money value 'That a man should always be able to support a woman financially' might seem OK at first glance. But if that value is stopping you from asking for a pay rise because you don't want to jeopardise your relationship, is it really OK? Or if it is preventing you as a couple from talking about investing and wealth creation together because one of you holds this money value, then again, is it OK?

Next, highlight the gems within your money values. Those values whose effects you want to start increasing.

If you don't have any positive gems, change your negative values to positive values. Or write down one or two positive money values you do want to have.

WHICH MEANS STARTING TWO NEW LISTS

1 The Unhelpful Wealth Creation Values you're carrying that you want to call out, to be aware of but ultimately diminish.

2 The Wealth Creation Values that are helpful to you that you want to take with you. Perhaps even include the money messages you don't quite have yet, but want to embed.

Now this is something we can work with. By becoming conscious of our money values we can start to challenge our behaviour because we understand why we're behaving that way.

Will it be easy? Absolutely not. That's because you've been carrying these money values with you for years. For some of you it's been decades. Which means they've formed a part of who you are.

That's OK.

Unf*cking your finances means turning on the light in the bedroom and choosing to get real. To get naked. You know that. We've talked about it.

Now it's time to do it.

Pop your goals and the money messages that are helpful to you, somewhere you can see them every day. Pop the unhelpful money messages on the reverse side so if you have a hiccup you can remind yourself what you're moving away from.

Then be aware of them as you move through this book, as you move through exercises, as you complete your 30-Day Financial Detox, and as you start to design the life you want.

"YOU'VE GOT TO VISUALISE WHERE YOU'RE HEADED AND BE VERY CLEAR ABOUT IT. TAKE A POLAROID PICTURE OF WHERE YOU'RE GOING TO BE IN A FEW YEARS."
SARA BLAKELY

be a goal digger

U p to now, we've been peering into the past and dissecting why you've ended up where you are now. Now, it's time to start looking forward and casting some vision. To start dreaming up some financial goals that you're excited about.

That's because looking forward is what's going to give you the excitement, the impetus and the motivation to unf*ck your finances.

That motivation starts with becoming a goal digger.

But let me warn you – for any goal cynics out there, I'm not talking wishy-washy goals here. And if you have thrown out goal setting because you are hopeless at New Year resolutions, let me tell you – I'm with you.

That's because I'm NOT a fan of New Year resolutions.

Let's be real – they're usually made while under the influence of too many champagne cocktails. They're often made because we feel pressure to change something, or because we want to offer up an answer to the inevitable question asked at New Year's Eve parties across the globe: 'What's your New Year resolution?' And the impetus for the resolution usually disappears as quickly as our champagne hangover.

Of course, there is often an element of truth to these resolutions. As human beings, we're captivated by the concept of a clean slate, fresh possibilities and a year where we're going to act differently, dammit! So, for a moment we buy into the magic of transformational change – but the desire to do anything about it usually fades as quickly as the smoke from the midnight fireworks.

Research consistently tells us that by the end of January the majority of us have all but abandoned all our New Year's good intentions.

Does this mean goals aren't worth it? Does it mean resolutions don't work? Are we destined not to change?

The short answer is, yes and no. If we carry on as we have done then of course goal setting won't work. That's because most of us are simply wishing, and what we quickly realise is there are no magical shoes, no Prince/Princess Charming or fairy godmother coming to save us.

I believe it's time to ask ourselves a different question. Instead of 'what do I want to change or achieve?', consider asking instead, 'what am I prepared to suffer for?'.

That's because making a New Year's resolution is easy.

I want to buy a new house, find a new job, start a business, pay off debt, lose weight, find a partner, travel, save more, retire, discover a magical pony that will sing sweetly to me each night. OK, so that last one may have been a tad ridiculous, but let's face it, it's all just a giant fantastical wish list at this stage.

Of course, not everyone ditches their New Year resolutions so quickly.

Some sign up to gym classes, hire a personal trainer, make an appointment with a financial planner or accountant, sign up to a dating website or set up online bank accounts so they can get serious about saving.

Often taking the first step is easy and kind of exciting. It's the second week of 6am starts to meet your personal trainer (when you're no longer on holiday!) when the suffering starts. Or dealing with sugar cravings at 4pm every day and trying desperately not to give in to the calling of a chocolate Hobnob. Or going out on two dates with total duds and feeling that it's just hopeless, so you cancel your eHarmony subscription. Or saying no to a day of shopping with girl-friends because you know your willpower won't hold out, only to find yourself sitting miserably at home with your social media powered up and clicking through to purchase.

That's when we start to figure out whether the goals we've created are worth it or not. By whether we're prepared to suffer to reach them. Which is why I believe we may as well deal with the suffering head on when we're making goals. Look it in the eye, decide if the goal is worth the pain, and make a plan for what we'll do when suffering rears its ugly head.

Whether your financial goal is to purchase an investment property, start a share portfolio, contribute the maximum to your personal pension, donate more to charity, start a business or holiday abroad, your first question should always be, am I prepared to suffer for it?

If it's a foreign holiday, are you prepared to not buy any new shoes this year? If it's buying a rental investment property, are you as a family prepared not to go on an expensive holiday and to cut down on extra-curricular activities for the next few years? If it's buying an asset or donating more to charity, are you prepared to suggest to friends that you get together for a barbecue, rather than cocktails at the trendy new wine bar that's just opened?

If the answer is no, either the goals are wrong and you didn't really want them or you need to do some serious work on your willpower!

Because if we want to achieve our goals we need to be sure they truly are our goals. Otherwise we're not going to suffer for them.

Too many of us make goals based on something we think we should want. Or something we're told we should want. Or something we feel expected to choose.

If your partner wants you to lose 10 lb and you don't, you're probably never going to lose the weight (unless you were to lose the 12 stones that is your partner). If you want to start a business this year, your suffering is probably going to include risk, sleepless nights and many 60–80-hour weeks with no immediate financial reward. If you're not interested in that you might want to reconsider whether you want to start a business. If you don't actually value long-haul holidays but simply feel expected to as part of your lifestyle, you may not be prepared to suffer for it.

The trick is to make sure your financial goals are YOUR goals and are aligned to your Wealth Creation Values, which are the exercises you completed in the last chapter. (If you haven't done them, head back now and complete them.)

So how do you make sure your goals are really YOUR goals?

It starts with designing the life you want.

This is how you not only start to become excited about your goals, but start to figure out what it is you want out of life.

Which is revolutionary.

Because some of you have never thought about designing the life you want. You've just mindlessly and unconsciously walked the path that is expected of you.

Designing the life you want means thinking about the future. Yes, that abstract thing you've stopped yourself from thinking about because it seems too vague and unclear.

TO MAKE IT MORE PALATABLE, I'VE BROKEN IT DOWN TO A FEW EASY STEPS:

STEP ONE THE FIRST STEP INVOLVES YOU DREAMING AND BRAINSTORMING.

Imagine you could create the future YOU desire. Not the future your parents, peers or friends want for you. The life YOU want. What does it look like? Where are you living? How are you earning a living? Who are you living with? What income are you generating? (Be specific.) What are you wearing? What do you look like? Pick a time period (preferably five or ten years). The more specific you can be the better.

Spend time thinking about these questions. Mind-mapping them. Jotting ideas down in your phone. Or just thinking. If you haven't thought about this before, it might take a few weeks. That's OK.

STEP TWO THE SECOND STEP IS TO WRITE IT DOWN.

Be specific and make it first-person. Choose your time frame (ideally five or ten years) and describe in detail what your future looks like. Make sure you're writing it from your point of view. From the point in time you're thinking of.

Be as specific as you can and write for as long as you want. Then read it back and make sure it excites you. If it doesn't, abandon it, think some more and start again.

If you're a picture person you might like to create a vision board as well, but I believe it needs to start with your words on paper first.

Once you have something written down, put it aside, then come back to it in a few days' time and read it again. Are you still motivated by it? How does it make you feel? Is it a life you're excited by?

That's how you start creating great resolutions. That's how you create motivating goals. By designing the life you want.

Why not just head straight to goal creation? Because short-term goals in particular are usually about putting out fires – or often they're what you think you should be doing. Your goals might be, 'save a deposit for a house', 'pay off my credit card debt' or 'consolidate my pensions'.

Sexy, right? Motivating, right?

Well, perhaps. But where it becomes sexy and motivating is when it captures you. When it excites you. When you know what you're working towards.

If you'd asked me a decade ago what my goals were, they were very short term. They were things like building my accounting business, paying myself a regular wage, figuring out where I wanted to live, saving for a house. All very safe and all great goals. But none of these things excited me.

After meeting my now-husband, we sat down and worked out what our lives might look like if we were to get serious, so to speak. And we both quickly realised we didn't want children. Which made us ask the question: if we don't want kids, what do we want our lives to look like?

That's where designing the life I wanted started for me.

A couple of years ago when I did this exercise, I realised that some of my goals are inherited goals. Still. Some of the goals I was carrying didn't excite me or motivate me, which was why I was self-sabotaging. When I figured out what I really wanted, when I figured out what I valued and what my personal mission was, suddenly my goals shifted slightly and I became excited about them again.

But it started with designing the life I want.

Now it's your turn to design the life YOU want, which means doing the exercise above.

Of course, the life I'm designing is going to be very different from yours. For now, it involves a home in the Blue Mountains and an apartment in the city, three businesses that are all about creating transformational change, three books, great relationships with an intimate group of friends, building a legacy, having influence, writing regularly and taking eight weeks' holiday every year.

Your goals might involve travel, business, corporate success, family success, sending your kids to the private school you went to, a sea change, a tree change, rebuilding from a relationship breakdown or starting a not-for-profit.

Once you've written down and dreamed up how you want your life to be (which is all that goals are) you've created a story of your future goals.

STEP THREE THE THIRD STEP IS ABOUT THE
PRACTICAL, THE PRAGMATIC. IT'S WORKING BACK
TO THE CURRENT DAY.

It's about taking the life you've designed, and working out
what that means for the next twelve months.

Because if you're drowning in credit card debt and the life
you want to design involves financial freedom, you need to
do something about that debt. If you're earning £40,000 a
year with no assets to speak of, and your goal is to live off a
investment income, you need to start saving and investing. If
your goal is to start a successful business but you're currently
working in a large company with a small hobby on the side,
you need to start learning about business.

Sure, it might seem unsexy and a little mundane, but if the
life you want to design is sexy then you won't mind suffering
for the next twelve months. Which brings us back to the
question we asked at the beginning of this chapter: 'What are
you prepared to suffer for?'.

Once you've worked out what your twelve-month goals are,
you may need to make sure they're helpful goals. Goals that
will take you closer to the life you're designing.

Which means putting each goal through its paces to make
sure it measures up.

Is your goal specific and measurable? Wearing heels more
often, losing weight, organising your taxes or making more
money in your business is too wishy-washy. Wearing suits
Monday to Friday for the month of June, losing 10 lbs by 30
September, paying yourself a weekly wage of £600 from next

week, working out your outstanding taxes and understanding how much is owed and organising a plan to pay off the debt by 31 December are specific and can be tracked.

Is your goal realistic? I'm 5'10", so if my goal is to be 6'2" then it's probably not going to happen (without the help of a really great pair of heels). Similarly, if your goal is to make sales of £1 million in six months and your last year's sales were £5,000 then you may need to sit down and do the maths to see if it's achievable. Of course, a stretch target is great – just make sure it's within the bounds of probability.

When is your deadline? Are you going to achieve success within a month, a quarter, six months, a year? Set a date and mark it in your calendar. I believe that a date as a deadline, such as Sunday 30 June, is much better than 'within six months'. It's tangible and it's not a moving target that you can keep restarting the clock with.

Remember, at this stage you're not figuring out the plan for how to make the goal a reality. You're just making sure the goal is true for you, that it's going to take you closer to the life you want and it's broken down to twelve-month goals that are realistic, specific and measurable.

Now it's up to you. Remember, this is the fun part. It's about dreaming (not wishing) and starting to design the life you want.

"Goals are dreams
with deadlines."
Diana Scharf Hunt

"THE SECRET OF CHANGE IS TO FOCUS ALL OF YOUR ENERGY NOT ON FIGHTING THE OLD, BUT ON BUILDING THE NEW." SOCRATES

dirty planning

You've done some amazing work so far. By now you should be starting to get a bit excited and – fingers crossed – are even wanting to really get stuck into it. But you're still a little unsure about what's next.

That's because the hole you've fallen into might be deep. There might be three forks in the road and you're scared of taking the wrong one. You're realising all these things about yourself and starting to take some power back, but you don't trust yourself.

Which is why it's time to roll up your sleeves and get busy planning how to get out of that hole, deciding which road to take and beginning to build that trust in yourself.

I know we've already talked about looking into the future, but let me remind you how rarely most people do that. Let me remind you how rare what you're doing is. I know, because I ask.

It doesn't matter if I'm hiring for a new position, talking to someone about money or working with someone to improve their business: I generally ask a very similar question. 'Where do you want to be and what do you want to be doing in twelve months' or three years' time?'

My estimate is that at least half the time the question is answered with a blank look, a non-committal shrug or a look of wonder, as the person says, 'I've never really thought about that before.'

Now, that's not you – because you've started to dream your big goals and you've started to break them down into 12-month goals. You've thought about the life you want to live and you've started to design it.

But let's be honest, you dreamed up big goals and the life you want to be living in five or ten years' time. You've worked out what your 12-month goals should be to move towards those big goals. But doing something about them? Creating a plan and then doing something about that plan?

That's where most people come unstuck. That's probably why you still need to unf*ck your finances.

Which is why the next step to remove some of that fog and start unsticking you is to become a dirty planner.

Now, I'm the type of person who loves lists, organising and strategy. My idea of foreplay is being asked to sit down and plan, which my husband well knows.

I'm the person who needs to have Communication Sundays, where I sit down with my husband and together we look at the week, plan what we're doing and where we're going to be. I'm the person who on 1 January sits down and works out how I'm going to have the best year yet and then forces my patient husband to do the same for our relationship. I'm the person who on a recent trip to Europe had a folder full of what to do, where to eat and a spreadsheet marked with what was happening on what day.

Yes, I know. It's sad.

I'm trying to understand the fact that not everyone feels the same way.

I also understand that for some people the idea of creating a plan for the next twelve months, broken into 90-day cycles, that deals with the practicalities of where you want to go, what you want to achieve and how you're going to make that happen can be a confronting one.

That's because it forces you to look at what might be, to question the what-ifs and perhaps face scenarios you're not necessarily comfortable with. It forces you to think about the actions that will turn your wish list into a reality. It also forces you to consider the real and perhaps uncomfortable steps you'll need to start taking to turn the 'wish' into the 'will'.

For some of you the wish list is much easier.

The dreaming is the fun part. It's nice to think about your future goals and the life you want to live, and you can roll them out if anyone asks what your goals are.

But doing something about it? Creating an action plan so that it happens? Then actually implementing that plan?

The thought makes many of you break out in a cold sweat.

Because some of you have been here before. You've made annual New Year resolutions and they've failed. You're also a little suspicious of the life you're trying to design. I mean, you don't have a crystal ball. Yes, you've done the goals exercise and have started designing the life you want, but the truth is many of you suspect the life you're currently designing may change.

Which makes you a little ambivalent about the planning and the doing. I mean, why bother if you don't honestly know where you're going to be in ten years' time?

I know if someone had asked me at age twenty where I wanted to be in ten years' time my answer would not have been where I was at age thirty. If you'd asked me at eighteen where I'd be at age thirty, I'd have told you I'd be married, a lawyer, first child at twenty-eight and second child at thirty.

Did all those things come true? Ummmm, no. And to be honest, thank God.

And, if you'd told my eighteen-year-old self that at age thirty-three I would be divorced, broke, the owner of an accounting firm and about to move into a shared house with a bunch of friends, I think I would have sat down and refused to keep going.

The same would be true if I'd asked the question of my twenty-five- or thirty-five-year-old self. Even though these were ages when I had started to think about and even do something about designing the life I want.

Yet even then the vision changed.

So why bother with goals and planning at all?

Easy. By thinking about your future, you ask yourself the hard questions and, if you're honest, confront what it is you really want out of life.

This forces you to think about what you value, what's important to you and why it's important to you. Which means you start to focus on that instead of the unimportant.

If you completed the exercises in the previous chapter, you'll be starting to design a life you're excited to work towards. That life may involve finishing a degree, changing career, only working thirty hours a week, starting a business, living abroad for six months every year, having children, buying a home or retiring at fifty.

Will you ultimately do all those things you planned? Who knows! What you can do, however, is plan for the financial eventuality. That way at least you have options.

Now, options are something I know many of you want.

Let's say your goal is to have children in three years' time, but you don't have a partner today. You can set out a plan for how you might achieve that. It might be joining dating sites, looking into IVF programmes or adoption agencies and finding someone who has already been there and done that so you can ask them what financial steps to include and what to avoid. Hopefully it will involve a financial plan for how you will be able to support yourself and a child regardless of whether or not a partner is involved.

Of course, if in twelve months or three years you've done the research and you've decided it's all too hard, you haven't met the right person to have a child with, or you want to wait another three years, no one is going to jump up and down and call you a failure. No good friend, that is. Instead, if you've stuck to the financial plan you created to have a child you will at least have created a pot of funds that will now give you options. Those options might be to travel for three months, start a business, change career or perhaps begin purchasing assets.

No matter what might ultimately happen, you've given yourself the gift of choice.

Which, again, is something I know most of you want. The financial freedom to have options.

WHAT ARE THE STEPS WHEN IT COMES TO DIRTY PLANNING FOR YOUR FINANCES? NOW THAT YOU'VE THOUGHT ABOUT WHERE YOU WANT TO BE AND WHAT YOU VALUE IN LIFE? NOW THAT YOU'VE STARTED TO DESIGN THE LIFE YOU WANT? NOW THAT YOU'VE BROKEN THAT DOWN INTO 12-MONTH GOALS?

It's about creating a step-by-step action plan for what you need to do to make those goals a reality. You can download the UK 90-Day Plan from themoneybarre.com.au and head to the Unf*ck Your Finances blog where all the exercises are stored.

1 **Write down your 12-month goals from the Goal Digger chapter.** Head back to that chapter and do the exercise now if you haven't yet.

2 **Break the year up into 90-day cycles.** For example, if you're doing this exercise in January your first 90 days will be January–March, second will be April–June, third will be July–September and last will be October–December. It doesn't matter when you start, just make your 90-day cycles begin from that point. If the perfectionist in you wants to wait until the first of the month or the beginning of a 'real' quarter, tell that voice to stop it and just start today.

3 **For each 90-day cycle work out the actions you'll need to take to achieve your goal within the 12 months.** For example, if your goal is to pay off all your credit cards within the 12 months and your current debt is £10,000, work out how much needs to be paid off each 90 days to achieve that

goal. If you're a seasonal worker then some of your 90-day payments may be higher than others.

4 **Download the 90-Day Plan and complete it for the current quarter.** Work out the specific actions you will need to take in the next 90 days to reach your goals. I'm also a fan of adding one or two extra action items. In the example above it might be automating the repayment so that every pay cycle the money is sent directly to your credit card. It might mean taking the cards out of your wallet and cutting them up. It might mean unsubscribing from certain shopping sites in order not to be tempted. It might mean transferring your credit card balance to an interest-free card. It might mean completing the 30-Day Financial Detox (yes, I'm going to nag you until you do it!). Your extra action items might include consolidating your many pension payments, challenging a direct debit expense or moving your savings from a bank account to a different type of investment. Make sure you have a list of actions and a start date and an end date for each one.

5 **Figure out how you're going to measure these actions.** These are milestones you can track each week to ensure you'll hit your goal in time. Your milestone might be a weekly saving of £50. Or your milestone might be ticking one-off action items by a specific date that, once completed, you won't need to do again – actions such as cancelling an online subscription, creating a will or organising a balance transfer from your current credit card to a zero-interest credit card.

6 **Work out how you're going to keep yourself accountable.** My tip is to tell people. Nothing makes you stick to a plan like having to admit to people that you've quit. Tell your partner, family, friends, colleagues, social media or blog about it. Then keep them updated.

7 **Celebrate every 90 days.** Perhaps don't celebrate by blowing a whole lot of cash, which will undo all the good you've done! But it might be going out for a cocktail with friends, buying a bottle of French champagne, or trying that new restaurant. At the beginning of the 90 days decide how you're going to celebrate so you have a carrot to keep you going.

8 **Start again.** At the end of the 90 days follow Steps 4–6 for the remaining three 90-day cycles. The trick is not to celebrate and stop, but to keep going. Each year you begin again with the Goal Digger chapter and then onto your 90-Day Plans.

Now, planning is great but it's only the first step. Often, the missing ingredient is action. It's fantastic to dream, to goal-set, to vision-board and to create 90-Day Plans – but these are only ever the first steps. Often they're the easiest steps, and perhaps the most fun, so we spend the most time on them.

But after we've dreamed it, planned it and talked about it – it's time to take some action.

When Alice fell down the rabbit hole she found a magic drink and a magic cake. Today, many of us are hoping for a magical financial solution to fall into our laps, but sadly it doesn't exist. Instead, it's up to you. Only you can start to unf*ck your finances and move on to create the life you want.

"IT IS OUR CHOICES, HARRY, THAT SHOW WHAT WE TRULY ARE, FAR MORE THAN OUR ABILITIES."

J.K. ROWLING, HARRY POTTER AND THE CHAMBER OF SECRETS

budgeting is a dirty word

B y now you've started creating some amazing foundations. You've started an action plan and are excited about the goals you're setting for yourself and what you're capable of achieving and building. Now we're going to look at how to start protecting all that hard work.

Which starts with figuring out where all that cash you're making is going.

The B Word. It's enough to make many of us break out in a cold sweat and flee from the whole idea of financially adulting.

That's because a budget is all about lack. It's about restriction. It's about being controlled by the fun police.

Or at least that's what many of us think.

What I want to suggest is that if you can change your thinking about money, you can actually reject the whole idea of a budget.

Don't believe me? Stay with me.

Let's think again about food. That's because I believe there's a natural synergy between money and food. The principles that apply to one often apply to the other.

Seth Godin, best-selling New York marketing guru and author, wrote a blog about food and serving sizes. Seth's concept is that our natural instinct is to 'fill up the bowl'. Our coffee, when we purchase it in our takeaway cup, is filled to the brim; our debt level is just below our credit limit; and we're taught to eat everything on our plate or to supersize to get more value for our money.

Seth's theory is that in order to deal with our natural inclination to fill our bowl we need to downsize it. If you want to do less of something, you need to get a smaller bowl.

Now this might seem like the simplest possible life hack, but I think it's genius because it's so easy to put in place. It just works. And it applies to so many areas of our lives.

If we apply Seth's concepts to losing weight we can literally change the size of the bowl or plate we eat from. So, if you want to drop a dress size you might change from a dinner plate to a smaller-sized plate. That way you're fulfilling your unconscious desire to fill your plate but you're also managing your portion size. Simply by changing the size of your plate.

Seth's hack works equally well when we apply it to how we manage our finances.

You can probably already start to think of examples. It's what happens every time we receive a pay rise. We're already used to dealing with a smaller bowl, yet when our bowl is made bigger by way of a pay rise it doesn't take long before our spending lifts to meet the new, larger income amount. Suddenly, we wake up one day and can't believe we could ever afford to live on our previous income level.

And we start searching for a bigger bowl.

How do we apply Seth's principle of a smaller bowl to our finances? Simple. We become savers by default, by limiting the amount we have available to spend. By effectively reducing the size of our spending bowl.

Sure, we could budget and work out exactly how much we have available to spend. Which I recommend you do for your fixed costs – such as home and car insurance, rates, utility bills, mortgage payments, rent and for your regular savings goal amount. This way you can be sure you've left enough for these essentials. (We'll look at how you do this in the following chapters.)

The problem with most budgets that include everything, including those non-essential things that there's a teeny chance we might want to spend money on, is that we generally inflate our spending amount. Just in case. We add a whole lot of things we'd like to spend money on, so our budget becomes a giant child's wish list instead of something that's helpful. We up the grocery amount, we add gifts, we include haircuts, beard trims, leg waxes, dog grooming and every other thing we think we couldn't possibly live without – and then wonder that there's nothing left at the end of the exercise to save.

Which is why we need to flip it.

Yes, we need to understand our fixed costs – but the rest? They can be included as you start using your bowls only if there is enough cash in the Everyday Bowl to spend on them. This Everyday Bowl is kept only for all these non-fixed items. (In the next chapter, we'll talk about the different bowls or accounts you should have, but stick with me here first!)

So, if your weekly wage is £250 and you're living at home with very few fixed expenses, then you might make your spending bowl £85 a week. If your weekly wage is £500, but your mortgage and regular bills are £300, you might choose for your spending bowl to be £150. This way you still have some forced savings, however small. You might argue that your life costs you more than £85 or £150. To which I say, fine. You can choose to eat everything and more on your plate every week – but is that going to get you closer to that life you were designing?

I didn't think so.

Of course, if your bills are large and your bowl is small you may need to figure out how to increase your income so that you have more options. This might mean taking a second job for a while, taking in a lodger, popping on your big-girl pants and asking for a pay rise, or starting a small business on the side.

Or perhaps you need to look at your fixed bills and ask if they really are fixed and if they're essential. It might mean asking yourself some hard questions, such as can you honestly afford the lifestyle you've chosen or do you need to downsize? Does it mean moving into a smaller apartment, selling the car with the loan attached to it, taking up running outside instead of renewing the gym subscription, getting new quotes for insurance, bartering haircuts with a girlfriend, taking your lunch to work or moving back home for a while to save money?

The reason I prefer the concept of a smaller bowl rather than a budget is because a budget is restrictive in the same way that dieting is restrictive. If you've ever tried a diet, you'll know that it may work for a time but you'll ultimately have a big blowout and it's all over.

Research supports this theory.

Professor Elaine Kempson is a Emeritus Professor from the University of Bristol, and an international authority on consumer financial issues with over thirty years' experience in conducting research and contributing to policy development. She confessed at the 2016 Good Shepherd Microfinance Financial Resilience Summit to being surprised by findings in her research that suggested budgets didn't work. She was going back to do further research into why, but I for one wasn't surprised. That's because we're far better at focusing on healthy eating than restrictive dieting.

Why should it be any different for our finances?

What does a no-budget world look like? How does this work practically? How can we apply Seth's concept to our day-to-day lives? How do we create a smaller bowl when it comes to our money?

WE'RE GOING TO LOOK AT THE EVERYDAY PRACTICALITIES, INCLUDING WHAT SHOULD GO IN EACH OF YOUR BOWLS IN THE NEXT CHAPTER. BUT HERE'S WHAT I BELIEVE THE BOWL CONCEPT SHOULD INCLUDE WHEN IT COMES TO OUR MONEY GENERALLY.

Automate. If we understand that our predisposition is to lift our spending to the income we're receiving, we can artificially reduce the money coming in by setting up automatic transfers to other accounts such as a savings account or a bills account. That way, the bowl that you have to spend from is much smaller and the challenge you need to accept is to only spend what is in your smaller account (and not to dip into your savings account.) We'll talk in detail about how to set up bank accounts to create smaller bowls in the next chapter.

Siphon off a pay rise. A pay rise means your bowl is automatically upsized, so before you get used to the extra cash hitting your bank account each month, make sure you increase your automatic transfer so that some of the pay rise is now being sent to your savings account. Again, you're taking control of the size of the bowl. If your pay rise means you're receiving an extra £100 per week, then increase your automatic savings transfer by an extra £50 and keep the extra £50 to spend.

Reduce the limit on your credit cards. For some of us, the danger of having a £5,000 limit on our credit card means that we automatically count that £5,000 as part of our spending money – or part of our bowl. If that's you, then take control by reducing the limit on your card to one you can pay off every month. That way, you're reducing the size of your bowl and reducing the funds you have access to for spending.

Reduce the number of credit cards. This is no different to reducing your overall limit. If you have two credit cards and a few store cards, then choose the card with the best terms, the best interest rate and cut all the other ones up. Or you might transfer the balance of all but one to an interest-free card and then cut all but one card up (including the interest-free card) so you're not tempted to spend. Too many cards can mean a far too generous-sized bowl, so reduce the temptation to fill it up by simply eliminating all but one.

Hide your savings. This is something I learned very early on about myself. If I was able to access my savings via my debit card then I considered them to be part of my bowl and

I'd spend them. Sure, you might argue I should work on my willpower and keep my savings attached to my card in case of emergency – but it was hopeless. Remember my chocolate compulsion? By understanding that's how I act, I become aware that hiding my savings is saving me from myself. If you're like me (which I know many of you are), then reduce the size of the bowl you can access on a daily basis by ensuring your savings aren't accessible. Perhaps they're not attached to a card or maybe, like me, they can't be accessed through internet banking. Work out how far removed they need to be and then don't touch them.

Know what's in your bowl. If you've ever been to an event where there's a buffet you'll see people come back to their table with a plate piled so high you'd swear it was their last meal. I know I've done it. As you pick through what's on the plate that you piled up in case you missed out, you wonder why on earth you chose sweet-and-sour chicken when you wouldn't normally eat it. You also catch other people pushing their food around wondering how so many random food groups ended up in their bowl. It's no different when it comes to our finances. I'm sure there are regular and irregular expenses coming out of your accounts that you didn't realise you were paying for, you've never used, have stopped using or even have no idea what they are. When you divide up your bowls you can start to have clarity around what should be in them, and you can be selective around what you spend your money on. And opt out of things you shouldn't be paying for.

Understand your natural instincts. You could, of course, work on your willpower, but if you're a shocking chocolate addict like me you'll understand that, if it's in the house, all the willpower in the world won't stop you from scoffing the entire bar by the time you go to bed. Manage your finances so your bowl is smaller, rather than beating yourself up for having no self-control when it comes to devouring the contents of the bowl.

What I love about Seth's concept is its simplicity.

By reducing the size of our bowl through a series of automatic payments, controlling our debt levels, hiding our income increases and putting our savings out of sight, we don't have to be permanently on alert for overspending.

Instead, it's about working with our natural inclinations, not fighting against them.

"MONEY IS ONLY A TOOL. IT WILL TAKE YOU WHEREVER YOU WISH, BUT IT WILL NOT REPLACE YOU AS THE DRIVER." AYN RAND

bank accounts 101

Hopefully you nodded along and now understand the concept of the smaller bowl. My guess is that it kind of made sense to you, but you're still not quite sure how it works in real life.

That's because often we're taught the theory, but we're rarely taught the practical.

I mean, think back to the classroom. We're taught so much theory at school that we've never actually put to good use in our daily lives. Trigonometry? The feudal system? Ancient Roman architecture?

Let's make it crazy practical when it comes to bowls, budgeting and bank accounts. Perhaps the simplest and most frequent financial question I'm asked is, 'How should I set up my bank accounts?'

Really.

That's because you're doing what you think is right but it's not quite working for you. And you're not talking about money with friends, so you're not learning from each other.

Which means you miss out.

Does how you're setting up your bank accounts honestly matter? Yes! It's important. Trying to manage with one or two bank accounts and remember how much you have, how much you need and not dip into your honeypot of savings is bloody hard. Because it relies on you being super-disciplined and having a deep insight into your finances.

Which we know by now isn't f*cking true.

Which means we need to sort ourselves out right now when it comes to the bank accounts we should hold.

The first thing to understand is that there is no one size fits all. Neither the number of accounts, the type or whether you can access them or not. It's about creating a system that works for you (remembering that the reason you picked up this book is probably because your current one doesn't).

HERE IS MY EASY-TO-FOLLOW GUIDE FOR THE BANK ACCOUNTS YOU MIGHT WANT TO CONSIDER AND HOW THEY WORK. WHILE IT MIGHT SEEM LIKE A LOT OF BANK ACCOUNTS, JUST REMEMBER IT'S ABOUT PROTECTING YOUR HONEYPOT OF SAVINGS AND MAKING SURE YOU REACH THOSE GOALS YOU'VE SET FOR YOURSELF.

The Everyday Account: This is the account your wages are paid into and from which you pay your everyday expenses. These expenses include groceries, nights out, clothes, gym membership, haircuts, movies etc. Money is transferred from this account to your other accounts. The idea is once money runs out of this account then you need to make do, be creative or start inviting yourself to relatives' homes for meals. So, if you want the shoes, go crazy. But it may mean you eat baked beans for the rest of the week.

To contribute per month: 100% of your salary (less if you can have your salary split up by your HR department and paid directly into your other bank accounts). How much will end up in your Everyday Account? Don't worry about that yet. It's important to figure out the other accounts and then work backwards. This means what you're left with in your

Everyday Account is all you have left, and the discipline I want you to build up to is to live to that! Now, if once you've allocated funds you don't have enough left in your Everyday Account to live the life you've become accustomed to, you have some decisions to make. You might try and reduce the amount and number of your bills. Either by trying to find a better deal, selling a car or downsizing. You might reduce the size and type of your holidays. You might reassess your goals and the time-frame you want to meet them. You might look for more income either through a second job or starting a business. Or you might decide to reassess your current lifestyle and how you're spending your money because your goals are more important. Whatever is left in the account is guilt-free spending for you.

The Bills Account: The reason I recommend a separate Bills Account is so you are allocating funds for these fixed expenses. The bills to include in this pot are your must-have or absolutely-necessary expenses. They include rent, mortgage repayments, heating, water, insurance, school fees and car payments. While I think, for example, a gym membership is great, it's not a must-have so don't include it here. Instead, that comes out of the Everyday Account, if you can afford it with what is left over.

To contribute per month: The first step is finding out how much your known and regular bills are and then annualising them. This means your weekly rent of £280 becomes £280 x 52, your electricity of roughly £350 per quarter is £350 x 4 and so on. The bills to include in this pot are your must-have or absolutely-necessary bills. Once you figure out the total amount, divide it by 12. This then becomes the amount you need to contribute to this account each month.

The Oh F*ck Account: This is the bank account for when financially derailing events happen that f*ck up your financial plans. It's meant to be used only if an unpredicted event occurs, such as a plumbing repair, an emergency medical bill or needing to replace your fridge. The idea of the Oh F*ck Account is so you don't dip into your savings for emergencies but have a built-in buffer.

To contribute per month: Work out how much you'd feel safe to have as a buffer (for example, £2,000, £5,000 – or, my recommendation is three months' wages). If you have that money sitting in another account already, transfer it here so you don't need to regularly contribute unless you use the funds. If you don't, then divide your oh f*ck amount by 12, 18 or 24 and this becomes your regular monthly amount to contribute.

The Holiday Account: This account is for your fun activities such as annual holidays so that, again, they're not ripped out of your Savings Account.

To contribute per month: Work out realistically how much you'd like for an annual (or bi-annual) holiday and divide it by 12. If you're not an annual holiday person but you enjoy taking mini-breaks, work out the total of this amount and then divide it by 12. If you want to have a cheap holiday one year and an expensive one the following year, average the total of the two holidays over 24 months. Of course, if you don't love holidays but want this to be for something else, then make it unique to you. But don't overdo it!

The Savings Account: Remember your goals? Your dirty planning? Those things you've decided are worth saving and suffering for? Whether it's your house deposit, your new business or private school fees, this account is for you to save specifically for that. The idea being that you don't ever touch these monies for anything else. Ever. This account should initially be a high-interest account, or if you have a mortgage, an offset account. If your goal is to pay down credit card debt, your Savings Account may be your credit card, which is cut up but regularly being paid off with your 'savings amount'. You may also have more than one savings account. For example, if some of your 'savings' are being paid to an investment such as a managed fund, ETF (exchange traded funds), direct shares or property then the total of these amounts is represented and broken up here.

To contribute per month: You should have already worked this out in your Goals and Planning chapters. If you haven't, head back there now.

IF YOU'RE A COUPLE

Individual accounts. I can't stress enough the importance of having money of your own. I also think the amount doled out to each of you should be the same. Regardless of who is earning the money. Work out how much you're going to have separately to play with and make sure the money is transferred to each of your accounts regularly.

The F*ck Off Fund. I'm once divorced so I'm a big fan of having your own F*ck Off Fund if you're sharing all your resources. This fund means you have the independence to leave and start again if you need to. It can also give you the security of knowing you never need to find any cash – which, strangely, makes you more secure in your relationship because you know you have a buffer.

Of course, if you choose not to pool your funds this set-up will be different. For example, my husband and I have worked out how much we need to contribute to our joint account for all our joint bills and entertainment. We have a joint account and a joint credit card and that's it. Yes, we also have different holding investments together but, as a couple, these are the only two bank accounts we share.

Separately, however, it's a different matter. We make sure we have the appropriate bank accounts that ensure we're saving for holidays, we have a small amount for the everyday and we have a buffer.

How you choose to organise your accounts will depend on whether you have only one person bringing in the income, if you got together early or later in life, whether you're part of a blended family and more.

What is important is that, somehow, somewhere, a system exists that is working for you.

Of course, setting up your bank accounts is only step one. The second and crucial step is automating the whole system of accounts so you don't f*ck with it.

The risk is that you might be tempted not to transfer money to your Bills Account one month because you really want to go on a girls' weekend away and don't have enough money in your Holiday Account, but plenty in your Bills Account. Until you realise a month later that the reason you had a lot of cash in your Bills Account was because your car registration and insurance were due. Or perhaps you don't transfer money into your Savings Account one month because it's Christmas and you want to buy gifts, and you miss January too because you want to hit the sales, and February you need to pay off your credit card so you skip it again.

See where the danger lies? That's right. The danger lies with leaving you in charge.

Which is why the most important step is automating your money management system through a series of automatic transfers so you can't f*ck with it.

Will this system need tweaking? Absolutely. You may have forgotten a crucial bill or, better still, you may downsize and end up needing less in your Bills Account. You might change the names of accounts so they suit you, and you might increase or decrease your Holiday Account because you had too much or too little in your Everyday Account.

Amending the automated amount is fine. Amending the bank account names is fine. Just make sure the system is ALWAYS automated.

That's because you can't be trusted. It's OK. I can't be trusted either. Which is why I use a great system.

What's next? Work out your amounts. Work out your accounts. Make a date at the bank. Set them up. Then automate them.

Boom!

"Decide what it is
you want
Write that shit down
Make a fucking plan
And
Work on it
Every
Single
Day."
Anon

"UNTIL YOU MAKE THE UNCONSCIOUS CONSCIOUS, IT WILL DIRECT YOUR LIFE AND YOU WILL CALL IT FATE." CARL JUNG

become a conscious consumer

I loved mystery stories when I was growing up and as an adult I'm still a fan. Puzzles, intrigue, true crime, a bit of online stalking.

If you're like me, this next chapter will be easy. If not, it's time to get your Nancy Drew on. It's time to become a detective and start taking an interest in what's going in and out of your bowls (or bank accounts.)

And it all starts with becoming a conscious rather than a sleepwalking consumer.

Let's begin with our online compulsions. Which means it's time for me to confess to a mild social media addiction.

Whether it's checking out what friends are doing on Facebook, tweeting during my favourite reality TV show or looking at fashion porn on Instagram, social media is a rabbit hole I all too frequently find myself falling into.

During my regular stalking, I mean scrolling, I'm often surprised by the energy given to outrage. Every day it seems I'm asked to sign a petition, share a hashtag or 'like' a page dedicated to fighting the latest cause.

Now, I'm not saying it's wrong to be passionate about important issues. Quite the opposite. But I wonder how often the average person likes, tweets, signs, shares or hashtags and then goes about their day unwittingly contributing to the very issue they've just railed about.

How would they do that?

Well, it's not because they're hypocrites. It's because they're unconscious consumers and aren't paying attention to where they're spending, borrowing and investing.

Now, you've already started working on turning this around by becoming aware of how you think and feel when it comes to money. You're starting to become aware of the money messages you're carrying, what your unconscious spending habits are and what you might want your goals to be.

It's now time to start becoming aware of what you're unknowingly contributing to when you're spending, investing and borrowing.

Huh?

Let's take it back to social media outrage. I believe if we truly care about the campaigns we are supporting, we need to become aware of how we may be unwittingly contributing to the very issues we're fighting. We need to realise our purchase power is just as, and perhaps even more, important than a signature on a petition. After all, most companies pay more attention to falling revenue than they do to online outrage.

Which means we need to take off our blinkers and start to become conscious consumers.

We can already start to see our blinkers being removed when it comes to food and fashion.

Jamie Oliver's food movement shone the light on how pigs are being treated. Jamie's intention wasn't to create vegetarians. It was for you and me to become informed and make educated choices. This has resulted in a demand for free-range products and a whole lot of informed consumers voting with their wallets.

Stella McCartney is a great example of someone pursuing ethical fashion. For Stella it's about how her clothes are made, who makes them, the conditions they work in, what they're paid and that no animal products are used in her clothing. In the West, our commitment to fast fashion means we have choices to make around how this is affecting our planet as well as how workers are treated.

Yet, for all the good we're doing with food and fashion we need to widen our view and start becoming conscious consumers with all our financial choices.

Which is a two-step process.

The first step involves taking off the blinkers and understanding the effect of your financial choices. The second step is critical and is all about tracking your spending so you own your choices.

STEP ONE BECOMING A CONSCIOUS CONSUMER MEANS WE START MAKING DELIBERATE AND INFORMED CHOICES ABOUT WHERE WE ARE SPENDING, BORROWING AND INVESTING.

Understand where your money is being invested. In life, you could be a card-carrying vegan who chooses what you eat and wear carefully and considerately. However, you could be inadvertently supporting companies that are pro-animal testing by not understanding where your money is being invested. Or you could be anti-tobacco because your grandfather died of lung cancer and, again, be unintentionally supporting tobacco companies via your investments.

And before you argue that you don't have any savings or investments, what about your pension?

Once upon a time too many of us ticked a box on a form and never gave it another thought. Before you spend valuable energy campaigning on social media, ensure you're not being outraged with one hand and participating with the other. You might argue that it's all too hard, and you don't understand what your fund is doing – but that's what your financial advisor or fund manager is for. Make an appointment and insist on having a list of exactly which companies your fund is investing in and what their activities are (make sure you understand that these companies may have, or be, subsidiaries).

Understand your spending. Before you add your name to another campaign featuring a child working too many hours in unsafe conditions, find out more about the supply chain in the stores you're spending money with. Because you could be signing today and inadvertently supporting companies who support child labour tomorrow. Yes, I understand this may involve a bit of time spent researching. But if you choose, every single week, to research one brand you're purchasing or one store you're buying from, then you can start to become a deliberate consumer. If you want to make life easy for yourself, choose local producers, smaller stores and ask the business owner directly where they source their product.

Understand your borrowing. Easy credit can make life, well, easy. But store cards, car loans, even being able to pay your insurance monthly, generally means your loan is being provided by a company you may not be aware you have a relationship with. Which means you might be choosing to shop with companies based on ethical values everywhere else in your life, but feel uncomfortable if you start to look at who you are now unconsciously providing profits to. I'm certainly not suggesting all these companies are unethical, but again it's about knowing who you're spending with and choosing whether to spend or not, according to your own values.

It's so easy to sign a petition, retweet a campaign or use a hashtag and then walk away feeling good about ourselves. The harder option is to spend some time researching where we're investing and spending.

STEP TWO BECOMING A CONSCIOUS CONSUMER AROUND YOUR WALLET.

Hopefully you've chosen to complete the 30-Day Financial Detox (you may as well just start it, I'm going to keep nagging until you do) and you're starting to realise there is a lot of spending happening that perhaps you don't intend. You may even be starting to catch yourself in situations where you're behaving in a way that runs counter to the financial goals, values and planning that you've done.

Becoming a conscious consumer is being aware of that and knowing what you're spending your hard-earned cash on.

So, while you're completing the detox, this is the perfect opportunity to start tracking and monitoring your spending. That way you can own the choices you make.

Personally, I spend way more than the national average on clothes and shoes. Way, way more. The thing is I'm completely OK with it. That's because I *choose* to spend way more on clothes and shoes. The difference is I know the figure I spend,

I know what I need to earn in order to spend that much, and I also know what I need to cut down on or go without in order to be able to afford it.

Which means I don't eat out at expensive restaurants as often as others. I rarely drink, so my alcohol bill is teeny-tiny when I do dine out. I don't go on long-haul holidays. I don't spend a lot of money on movies and expensive entertainment because I'd rather read a good book that I can buy at my local secondhand bookshop.

And I track my spending.

Which is what Step Two is all about. It's about downloading one of the apps listed at the end of this book and giving it a go. If you don't love it then download another until you find one you do like. There are free options and paid options, so this isn't a barrier. You can use all of them on your mobile phone, they can all upload your bank statements, and they're super-easy to operate.

Then, each week it's about allocating your spending and every month sitting down with a glass of wine and working out where you went right, where you went wrong, what tripped you up, what worked for you and what you need to adjust next month. It's about looking at your spending, at the amounts you've allocated to different accounts during the month, and asking yourself if you're comfortable with how much you've spent. It's about taking the time to recognise, cancel and change subscriptions you haven't opted out of because you forgot about them.

It's like jumping on the scales every week and then each

month figuring out what you need to adjust with your food and your exercise. Sure, you could do without it, but you won't know how you're tracking with your weight goals if you don't.

It's exactly the same for our finances.

Becoming a conscious consumer is about starting to own what you're doing financially. It's opening your eyes to the decisions you're making on a daily basis and owning them. It's about choosing to adjust your behaviour as a result, because your values and your goals are worth it. It's being mindful about your spending and the effects of your choices so your eyes are wide open to the consequences rather than restricting yourself to a limiting budget.

Tracking is key.

Without it you can't be informed, you can't make great choices and you can't, hand on your heart, know what is going on with your hard-earned cash.

You might be shocked at how much you're spending on some things. You might be outraged to know just what your investments are supporting.

That's OK. Actually, it's great. As long as you do something about it.

So pick an app, download it, begin using it and start becoming a conscious consumer.

"You can't hit a home run unless you step up to the plate. You can't catch a fish unless you put your line in the water. You can't reach your goals if you don't try."
Kathy Seligman

"THE SHOE THAT FITS ONE PERSON PINCHES ANOTHER; THERE IS NO RECIPE FOR LIVING THAT FITS ALL CASES." ELEANOR ROOSEVELT

remove yourself from temptation

You've started the 30-Day Financial Detox and begun the process of working out how you think, what your goals and your values are. You've begun to plan and create your 90-day actions. You've started to organise and set up your bank accounts and automate your bowls. You've downloaded apps and are beginning to track your spending and become a conscious consumer. But there's still one problem, one pest that until you tame it and train it will continuously try to sabotage you.

That pest is YOU!

Don't believe me? Let's revisit my own serious lack of will-power. Yes, that's right, my name is Melissa Browne and I am a chocolate addict. Which you already bloody know.

Seriously, I just need to receive sponsorship from Cadbury or Lindt and turn this problem into a solution.

Hopefully what you've realised by now, simply by how much I've banged on about it, is that I have absolutely no willpower when it comes to chocolate.

The difference between me and most people is that I own my daily chocolate fix. I work within the constraints of someone with no willpower and I control the effect it has on my waistline by limiting the amount and type of chocolate I consume. I also begrudgingly exercise regularly because I don't want my regular chocolate intake to mean I can no longer fit into my large wardrobe of clothes.

And I eat craploads of chocolate – happily and guilt-free.

I believe that many of us need to apply that same thinking to our finances.

That's because although most people are entitled to have a credit card, not everyone should. They also shouldn't have store cards, personal loans, payday loans, car loans or ever-increasing mortgages.

The truth is not everyone can handle credit.

If you know your credit card (or cards) will always be at their limit, then perhaps you need to rethink whether you should have them at all.

There's no shame in admitting you can't control how you deal with credit. It's simply acknowledging that you have no willpower when it comes to the extra funds and controlling the effect this has on your finances and your long-term goals. Or perhaps you can have a card, but it has a very small limit – and it doesn't live in your wallet so you can't be tempted to overspend. Or you can have a mortgage but it's not as large as what the mortgage broker told you it could be.

If you know you'll dip into your savings if a bright, shiny thing comes along, then protect your savings so you can't.

There's no shame in admitting that you struggle to save. It's simply acknowledging that you often end up dipping into the honeypot because you have no willpower when it comes to resisting bright, shiny things. And then setting up your accounts and investments accordingly. This might mean detaching your savings from your credit cards as you pay off debt. Or you might decide to take more extreme action and lock up your savings in a longer-term investment or in an account that you can't access within 24 hours.

If you know you're tempted to spend if you're bored, whether it's on social media or wandering around at lunchtime, then change your behaviour.

There's no shame in acknowledging your willpower is less than perfect. The problem arises when you don't adjust your behaviour and remove the temptation. This might mean 'unliking' and 'unfollowing' those retailers or brand influencers who are tempting you to shop. It might mean unsubscribing from newsletters and texting 'stop' to sale alerts. Or if you know that your 'window-shop' at lunchtime inevitably turns into a 'window-buy', it might mean leaving your wallet back at the office.

Sensing a pattern here?

All I'm suggesting you do with your finances is what I'm doing with my chocolate consumption.

Which means working out financially, how to ensure you don't have money in the pantry for you to gorge.

How do you do that?

Remember our smaller bowl conversation back in budgeting? Step one is figuring out your bowls, working out how much should be in each of them and then automating the whole system.

The second step is just as important.

It's placing a guard rail, or for some of you a booby-trapped electric fence, around those bowls to protect you from yourself.

What are guard rails?

To be honest, you've probably not consciously noticed them. They're the fairly unattractive but usually inconspicuous railings that protect us when we're driving or walking around areas that aren't considered safe. I'd probably go so far as to say we probably don't value them. We understand their purpose but we don't give them a lot of thought unless they're big, looming and unattractive.

The same marketing guru who came up with the smaller bowl concept, Seth Godin, also suggests that we demand guard rails.

In his blog Seth writes: 'It's tempting to believe that left to our own devices, we'll all maximise our health, make smart investment decisions and generally follow our instincts on the road to happiness. But it turns out that cigarettes are addictive, that financial distress causes people to make short-term decisions that are damaging, and that we even have trouble doing smart and easy things with 401k [tax-efficient savings in the US].'

You might not agree with Seth.

In fact, if you're a civil libertarian, or you are frustrated by obstructed views and legislated bike helmets, you'll perhaps vehemently disagree. For my part, I agree with him. I believe many of us need guard rails, but we rally against them because we believe that, as fully functioning adults, we shouldn't need them. Guard rails make us feel like children and some of us find that demeaning because we should be able to 'adult'.

To that I say – get over it!

That's because if we change our perspective, if we understand how we behave if left to our own devices, we'll see that guard rails aren't meant to merely restrict but, rather, their purpose is to give us back freedom.

You see, if you just relax against the guard rail, you can enjoy the view without needing to be so conscious of the risk. The guard rail allows you to drive to your destination without being fearful of the drop-off on the side, or the articulated lorry on the other side of the road, because there's a barrier. The guard rail allows us to be fully present without constantly needing to scan or take unnecessary risks.

How do you put a financial guard rail in place?

Easy. You become accountable. You put in place rules and boundaries for yourself.

Not because you're forced to, but because you've worked out where you want to go and you're determined to get there. You've worked out your values, your goals, your priorities – and, suddenly, the guard rails are necessary to help keep you on the path you've determined.

In short, you learn to love the guard rails because they allow you to concentrate on speed, skill and arriving where you want to go.

WHICH ALL SOUNDS GREAT IN THEORY – BUT WHAT DOES A FINANCIAL GUARD RAIL LOOK LIKE IN REAL LIFE? HOW DO YOU CONSTRUCT ONE?

1 **Work out where you want to go.** You've already done this by figuring out your short-term (twelve months) and medium-term (three to five years) goals.

2 **Work out your values and priorities.** Again, you've hopefully already done this by figuring out what you value and by doing your dirty planning.

3 **Work out how you currently operate.** This is the chocolate conversation, which you've started to think about with money mindfulness. It's all about figuring out how robust your guard rail needs to be. Because if your credit card debt is sky high, and you have shoes for days but no assets (and yet you desperately want to own your own home), then there needs to be some kind of mechanism created to protect you from yourself! This is where you get naked and real about how you react to and deal with money.

4 **Set up a new way of operating.** This is the structure of your guard rail. It will involve setting up your different bank accounts (or bowls), organising your direct debits so they're automated, downloading and using spending/tracking apps so you're monitoring your spending, hiding accounts from your internet banking systems, unsubscribing from shopping sites and taking credit cards out of your wallet. It might also involve putting up pictures of the view you're hoping to see (which in Step One is where you worked out you wanted to go) in order to keep you motivated.

5 **Check your speed.** Guard rails are fantastic, but they're not designed so that you can start driving at a hundred miles an hour. Make sure you regularly check how you're going with a daily, weekly, monthly, quarterly and annual check-in. This might mean that every day you're updating your app, every week you're checking your bowls, every month you're making sure you're on track with your goals, and every 90 days you set up a new plan for the next quarter to make sure you're on your way to achieving your long-term aims.

6 **Organise accountability.** In addition to putting up guard rails we can also employ a police force to regulate our behaviour. Your accountability might be with your partner, a friend, a mentor or a professional advisor such as myself. We have created a programme in our financial planning firm called The Mini Barre is designed just for this purpose. The important thing is that someone is keeping tabs on what you're doing and has permission to call out your behaviour if it doesn't align with what you want to achieve.

7 **Start driving.** Once everything is set up, guard rails are in place and accountability is organised, it's time to start. Which seems simple but it's often the missing final step. It's easy to create vision boards and work on mindsets. We also understand the psyche behind direct debits, lowering our credit card limits and investing. But too few of us are doing it. For many of us, it's time to get in the car and head off.

It's not rocket science, is it? Anyone can do it.

So why aren't you?

If you're really honest with yourself, if you really get naked and vulnerable, you know how tough this guard rail needs to be. How robust. You know how you operate, so just get f*cking real about it and stop sabotaging your future.

Set up your bowls, think about what guard rails you need to put in place and start saving yourself from yourself.

"The biggest human temptation is to settle for too little."
Thomas Merton

"GIVING UP ON YOUR GOAL BECAUSE
OF ONE SETBACK IS LIKE SLASHING
YOUR OTHER THREE TYRES BECAUSE
YOU GOT ONE FLAT." ANON

the weigh-in

I know someone who underwent a 12-week weight loss programme and every Wednesday she had to weigh herself to find out how she was progressing. Now I'm sure that works for some. Let's face it, if your goal is to lose weight then you have no choice but to weigh yourself regularly to make sure your exercise and meal plans are working and that you're staying on track.

Personally, I would hate it. I don't have a great relationship with scales and have consciously not weighed myself in over a decade. However, I do check in by occasionally trying on a pair of trousers I've owned since I was twenty-five. So there is still monitoring being done; it just doesn't involve scales.

What is important is that I'm making some type of regular assessment of my weight and/or size.

This assessment may be for no other reason than to determine if I'm going to have to buy a new wardrobe next season because I'm a size bigger than I was a year ago. (Trust me, my hip pocket can't afford that type of expense.)

It's also important to have a regular monitoring system with your finances. Just like a regular weigh-in, the form this takes is up to you.

For some it might be a daily check of your spending app to make sure there have been no blow-outs and you know how much you have available in your Everyday Account so you can adjust accordingly. For others it might be reading your Wealth Creation Values and looking at your goals while you brush your teeth each morning so you're motivated to stay strong and not self-sabotage.

What's important is that you create a system of check-ins so that you can monitor your progress and make sure you stay on track.

Why bother? If I don't monitor my weight it might mean having to buy a new wardrobe – but if I choose not to monitor my finances, the results can be far more costly.

Let's take Sonja Smith (totally made-up name, but comprised of many clients I've met or worked with over the years). Sonja is super-excited when she starts out. She understands her values, she's started the 30-Day Detox and she's going to head to the bank at lunchtime on Friday to set up the accounts. Then she'll figure out the apps. But Friday was crazy busy at work, so she didn't get to the bank and went out with girlfriends for cocktails that night, which meant she needed to grab some new shoes after work. On Saturday she downloaded the app but was too hungover to make sense of it, so she put it off until Sunday when she unexpectedly hooked up with girlfriends for brunch. Fast forward six months and she's done nothing. In fact, she's gone backwards because she never really hit start!

Or Sally Smith. Who completed the 30-Day Detox, did all the exercises, downloaded the apps, used them for two months, found she was gaining some traction and then stopped. Because she figured she was OK now. Guess how long Sally's momentum lasted when left to her own devices and willpower? If you guessed less than thirty days you were right on the money. Which meant in less than a month she'd undone all her hard work.

You see, the problem with not having any sort of checks, balances and weigh-ins is that your financial future is left solely up to YOU!

Which we both know is madness.

Instead, make life easier for yourself. Create a series of regular weigh-ins so you can ensure you're moving from financially unf*cked, to financially resilient to financially well. And you stay there.

WHAT DOES A REGULAR WEIGH-IN LOOK LIKE?

Daily. It's a great idea on a daily basis to just take a peek at your tracking app. That's because you may be surprised at how much lunch cost yesterday and how much it depleted the pot. Or you may be surprised by an amount that has been deducted from your credit card that seems like a regular monthly amount and you're not even sure what it's for. It gives you the opportunity, particularly when you first start out, to stay on the front foot and keep your financial intentions in the front of your mind. I also think it's a great idea to look at your Wealth Creation Values and Goals daily to remind yourself what you're working towards. Maybe save them as the screensaver on your phone, or pop them on your bathroom mirror as a daily reminder.

Weekly. This is your weekly weigh-in so you can assess, monitor and adapt. It means looking at your action plan, checking to see if you're on track with what you said you were going to do, checking your spending on your app and making sure you're comfortable with where and how you're spending, and making sure you have enough in your different bowls. It's the opportunity to adapt, to change your behaviour and to make minor tweaks as you go, rather than getting to the end and giving up because you didn't adjust sooner.

Monthly. This is where you weigh yourself against the milestones you set in your 90-day plans. At your monthly check-ins you should be able to really see how far you've come and start to see yourself making some inroads in the goals you've set and your 90-day plans. Check how much you're spending in your apps, check your goal tasks and milestones on your 90 day plans and make adjustments as you need.

90 days. This is the big one. Put aside a couple of hours every 90 days and assess how you went over this period. Celebrate if you achieved what you wanted to achieve or figure out what went wrong if you didn't. Then set your next 90-day plan in place and start again.

Annually. Take the time every year to go through the whole process again. What are your goals, your money values, your long-term plan, the whole shebang. If you're in a relationship I absolutely recommend doing this together so that you're on the same page and you're both working together towards a common purpose rather than pulling apart. If you have kids, let them know the part they can play and give them ownership over some of the plan. That way the whole family is working together and your children are building great financial foundations themselves. If you have a strong friendship group, why not do this together so you can support each other and keep each other accountable.

At the end of the day, it's about creating great financial habits that will replace the unhelpful ones you've carried with you up to now.

Whether we compare it to a weight check-in or wanting to run a marathon, the end result is the same. Whenever you're starting a long-term process you need to build in a series of check-ins so you know if you're on track.

Still not convinced? OK, let's compare it to wanting to run a marathon instead.

My co-founder at The Money Barre, Lauren, gets up at 5:30am every day and either runs or goes to the gym. I admire her dedication and each week I tell myself that I should start exercising in the morning before the length of time I spend at work wears me down and stops me doing something at the end of the day. Of course, I'm not a morning person (really, really not a morning person) and so any exercise before I start work simply never happens. And unfortunately, I don't get any fitter by thinking I should do it.

The difference between Lauren and me is she has created a daily habit that means every day she is ensuring she exercises. I'm sure she doesn't enjoy getting up as early as she does and would rather sleep in some mornings, but she generally has some type of long-term goal she's working towards, which have included half-marathons, marathons, 50km trail runs and more. So she simply does it.

Often we set lofty goals and things we want to achieve, then before long the daily grind sets in and it becomes too hard and we quickly lose focus.

But athletes don't get to the Olympics by crossing their fingers and wishing, or by waking up in the morning and deciding it's too hard and hitting the snooze button. Instead, they set up a series of daily habits, weekly rituals, monthly check-ins and annual goal sessions that cover everything from when they get up, what they repeat to themselves before a race, what time and how often they train, what they eat and perhaps even the underwear they wear. It's all designed to create a series of habits to help ensure success and the achievement of their long-term goals.

Interestingly, all athletes don't have the same habits and rituals to help them succeed. There isn't a secret formula for success that would ensure all Olympic athletes would succeed if they adopted this training regime, or that eating pattern, or a combination of both. Instead, it's about them figuring out what will work best with their particular bodies and psyches, their sport, their goals and their timetables and then having the discipline to see it through.

It's the same for us mere mortals.

Too often clients see me and want the magic pill or formula that will guarantee success – but, sadly, there's no such thing.

Instead, the unsexy side to finance is setting up a series of weigh-ins, check-ins, markers and checkpoints so you know you're on your way to achieving your financial goals. So mark the weigh-in points in your diary and make a regular financial date with yourself.

"THE ONLY MAN WHO STICKS CLOSER
TO YOU IN ADVERSITY THAN A FRIEND
IS A CREDITOR." ANON

the good, the bad & the ugly of debt

Debt. How to pay it off quickly, how to get rid of it, how to leverage it, how much of it to have – I've been asked every type of question you can imagine about debt over the years.

I've sat with families, singles, young couples and older couples who have been saddled with mountains of debt. Who spend a large chunk of their income simply trying to keep up with their interest payments, never mind trying to reduce their debt and get ahead. Who are in utter despair over it and are deeply ashamed that they can't keep up.

Which means I get that for many of you debt is a big issue.

So how do you get rid of it? Should you pay debt off quickly? How much debt should you have? Is debt ever OK?

In a time of low interest rates, it's easy to be swept up by the notion that we need to pay all our debt off as quickly as possible. Particularly if we've just gone and purchased a property and have the massive mortgage to go with it, or if we're about to borrow to invest in property, shares or funds.

But what if I was to suggest to you that paying all your debts off at once is not as smart as you think?

Some people have been taught that all debt is bad and it's essential to get rid of it as quickly as you can. However, it's important to understand the different types of debt you have – because while some debt might indeed be bad debt, some debt is actually good debt.

It's a strange concept I know, but stay with me while I explain.

Let's say you have a mortgage on your home of £300,000,

an investment loan of £400,000, credit card debt of £10,000, a student loan of £15,000 and a car loan of £10,000. Most people would generally be making at least the minimum principal and interest payments on all these loans, which means each individual debt is gradually reducing each year.

Now, gradually paying down all these loans might seem like a reasonable solution. However, when we understand the difference between good debt and bad debt we can make strategic decisions around what should be paid down faster and, perhaps, what debt shouldn't be paid down at all.

This might seem an odd concept but it's one that can save you potentially tens of thousands of pounds (or more) in the long run. And help quicken the process of unf*cking your finances.

SO HOW DO YOU KNOW IF WHAT YOU HAVE IS GOOD DEBT, BAD DEBT OR OK DEBT? WHAT DEBT SHOULD YOU BE PAYING OFF AND WHAT SHOULD YOU BE PAYING INTEREST-ONLY ON OR MAYBE EVEN MAKING NO REPAYMENTS AT ALL?

Bad debt. Bad debt is generally any type of debt that you won't receive a tax deduction for. So in the example above it would be the mortgage of £300,000, the credit card debt of £10,000 and potentially the car loan of £10,000.

Of course, just because all these debts are bad debts doesn't mean they're all equally bad. It's important to look at your bad debts and work out which ones should receive the most attention in the form of extra repayments, rather than just paying them off at the same rate.

How you determine which is bad debt and which is worse debt is by looking at the loans themselves.

For example, the mortgage of £300,000 might seem the scariest because it's the biggest, but if it's at an interest rate of 5% and your credit card debt of £10,000 is at an interest rate of 15% then it makes sense to pay the credit card debt off first. This would mean paying the minimum onto the mortgage and diverting any extra savings onto your credit card debt, and then cutting your credit card up, or at the very least taking it out of your wallet! For some of you it may mean transferring your credit card balance to an interest-free card and paying the minimum amount each month that will ensure the card is paid off within the interest-free period.

Credit card debt is the worst type of debt so it's important to make a plan to pay it off quickly. Once that's done make sure they're at a limit you can handle and can repay in full monthly. If you're struggling with credit card debt it's sometimes cheaper to consolidate them with a loan that has a lower interest rate or engage a professional to negotiate a payment plan. What is critical is that once you've accomplished this, you need to ensure you don't get into trouble in future by deciding to say no to credit and opting to have a debit card instead.

Of course, once the credit card debt is under control and the car loan is being paid off regularly (or the car sold, the large debt paid off and a cheaper car purchased if that's more appropriate) then you might divert your attention to repaying your home loan faster. Particularly if you have an eye-wateringly large mortgage.

OK debt. If the car loan of £10,000 was for a certain type of vehicle that is essential for your work, then this loan may convert from bad debt to OK debt. Now, I call this OK debt rather than good debt because it's for an asset that is going to depreciate in value, so you still want to pay it off. However, if you have a mortgage, credit card debt and other loans it makes more sense to make additional repayments to your bad debt first, rather than making additional repayments to your OK debt.

Student debt can be OK debt, as the interest rates are between 3.1% and 1.5% (based on RPI), depending on when you studied. You also only pay it back once you are earning over a certain threshold. It just makes more sense to pay the credit card, car loan and mortgage off first (as the higher the interest the quicker the debt grows) than to make additional repayments here.

In some cases, your mortgage might fall in the OK debt category, particularly if you're going to retire in a few years time and you're still working. That's because with the current low interest rates, it may make more sense for you to make the maximum pension contribution and receive a tax break than to be making extra contributions to your home loan. Of course, once you retire you can then withdraw these extra super contributions in a lump sum and dump them straight onto your home loan.

Good debt. Tax-deductible loans can always fall into the category of good debt, which in our example is the investment loan of £400,000. I find that people usually want to reduce this loan fast because it's a big loan and they want to own their investment debt-free. But the interest on this loan is a tax deduction, which means it's almost always cheaper than your home loan. So, if you have a mortgage on the home you're living in then you should almost always pay this one down first. Please check the HMRC government website for the most up to date advice here, as some rates are changing.

If you still have bad debts then it generally makes sense to convert good debts like investment loans to interest-only loans to maximise any interest claim you can make. It might seem strange to not want to pay off a loan – of course you want to reduce your debt, right? However, this strategy makes sense if you take the extra monies you save by switching to interest-only and putting them towards your bad debt. That way the entire debt amount is still reducing, but you are maximising any tax advantages you might have.

Interest and switching. What's important to understand is that even if you don't feel in control of your debt, you should be. Which means throwing loyalty out the window and starting to look out for numero uno.

How you do this is by checking your interest rates regularly and being prepared to switch.

One of my clients does this regularly with her business and investment loans and it drives one of my accountants crazy. But it's always worthwhile. Every couple of years she takes her loans to a mortgage broker or does her research to find out if she can get a better deal. And guess what? Every time she does it she wins. Sometimes it means she needs to take all her accounts and loans over to another bank. Which if she's saving 0.5% on, say, £700,000 worth of loans is a saving of £3,500 per annum. Or sometimes it means the bank she's currently with will match the rate that she's been offered. The one who ultimately wins every single time is her. All because she's prepared to spend a few hours doing her homework.

It doesn't matter if it's a credit card, insurance deal or your largest interest component – your mortgage. Make sure that at least every two years (every twelve months is better) you shop around to check you're getting the best deal. There are great sites online that will help you with this and I've listed some in the back of this book.

Of course, some people I talk to are amazing at paying off debt but are terrible at saving. Which means for them, debt is actually OK. That's because if left to their own devices, although they wouldn't save, there's no way they would miss a mortgage repayment.

Once again, it's important to understand how you behave, as well as understanding how you should be paying off your debt. That's because all debt is NOT created equal.

"BUT WHAT I HAVE REALISED OVER TIME IS THAT IN MANY WAYS, MONEY SPELLS FREEDOM. IF YOU LEARN TO CONTROL YOUR FINANCES, YOU WON'T FIND YOURSELF STUCK IN JOBS, PLACES, OR RELATIONSHIPS THAT YOU HATE JUST BECAUSE YOU CAN'T AFFORD TO GO ELSEWHERE. LEARNING HOW TO MANAGE YOUR MONEY IS ONE OF THE MOST IMPORTANT THINGS YOU'LL EVER DO. BEING IN A GOOD SPOT FINANCIALLY CAN OPEN UP SO MANY DOORS. BEING IN A BAD SPOT CAN SLAM THEM IN YOUR FACE." SOPHIA AMORUSO, #GIRLBOSS

should I buy a home?

few years ago I conducted research to discover what motivated people financially. I was surprised to find out that the top two things we want from our money are freedom and options.

The reason I was surprised is because I expected 'owning my own home' to be top of the list. But it seems that while it is important (it was number three), above it sat the freedom to have options.

I was taken aback by these findings because many of us pay lip service to wanting freedom and options, but how we behave with our money tells quite a different story.

Perhaps it's because home ownership is such a deeply ingrained part of our culture. Or because we feel home ownership is a rite of passage and we haven't truly grown up if we haven't yet achieved it. Or perhaps we believe home ownership fills the need to provide a safe and secure place for our family.

Whatever the reason, I'm finding that our behaviour when it comes to bricks and mortar is in opposition to our strong desire for freedom and options.

As a financial advisor, more and more I'm seeing couples who are seeking a huge mortgage to secure the home of their dreams. Even scarier is that, too often, I'm hearing arguments that interest rates will stay low for years and even decades to come and property prices will only continue to rise.

Which are dangerous suppositions to hold as truths.

Now, I'm not against owning your own home. I've owned my home for all but a few years since I was twenty and have generally made money from home ownership. However, at the beginning of this book we talked about how the script was changing. How what got us here won't necessarily get us there. Which is why it's important that we stop subconsciously doing what has always been done. Instead, it's about doing the sums, working out your goals and working out if home ownership is right for you.

There's already a growing number of young people who are questioning whether they should even bother trying to own a home. With the price of properties rising and median home prices in some suburbs well out of reach of many potential first homebuyers, it is certainly a dream worth reconsidering.

The problem with the alternative, however, is when you're not accumulating any assets of your own. That is, unless you consider a third option, which is renting where you live and buying property as an investment.

This third option is an interesting alternative and one worth considering if you are able to remove the emotion around owning your own home.

So what are the arguments both for and against owning your own home?

THE CASE FOR BUYING YOUR OWN HOME

Emotion, pure and simple. The first and most obvious argument for home ownership is that you own the family home. For some people this is still their number one goal, even after all the exercises and values lessons, so it has to remain as number one on the emotional hit list.

Stability. Being a perpetual tenant means you are at the whim of your landlord, who may decide to sell the property, renovate it or move into it themselves. That's why if stability is important to you, home ownership will be attractive.

Improvements you make will (hopefully) increase the value of your property. Many people like to put their own stamp on a place. If you're renting, any material changes often can't be taken with you when you go. Whereas if you own your own home, improvements will hopefully increase the value of the property, presuming of course that you haven't overcapitalised.

Capital Gains Tax. This is often a game-changer. Owning your residential property makes it a Capital Gains Tax-exempt asset. This means when you sell your home you won't pay a penny of Capital Gains Tax on the profit. It's a big one and, for as long as it exists, will always make home ownership attractive.

Using the equity. Once you've paid off your mortgage you can use the equity to fund investments, business and more. Banks love bricks and mortar as security and you can generally borrow more, and at a cheaper interest rate. Of course, if you have an investment property this will still be an option.

Once you've paid off your mortgage, that's it. Unlike rent, which you'll pay forever (unless you squat or live with Mum and Dad), once you pay off your mortgage that large regular expense is gone. Which means if you are strategic and purposeful around paying your debt down quickly you can then apply these funds to building other assets.

THE CASE AGAINST BUYING YOUR OWN HOME (BUYING AN INVESTMENT PROPERTY INSTEAD)

Opportunity to buy in a different area. If you live in an expensive city, it may be that your money is best invested elsewhere. Perhaps there is an area where property is more affordable and will deliver a better return on investment, earning a higher yield and with more chance of a capital gain. And you never know, you may end up moving there yourself when you want more space!

You are not tied down to one asset. There is a growing trend, especially among younger people, not to be tied down for years to one location. They want to experience multiple locations or be able to move if their job requires it. Renting your home and owning an investment property instead means you're still building wealth through property, but you're not restricted to the one location.

You don't have to pay maintenance costs, and if you do they may be a tax deduction. As any home-owner will tell you, the purchase price is only the start of what a house will cost you. There are the costs to maintain your property as well as the costs to upgrade as things wear out. If this is your home there is no tax deduction, but if it's your investment property you may be able to claim these costs either in full or over a number of years.

You need to sell your home to realise your gain. Many people may tell you, quite proudly, how much their home has gone up in value and how much equity or profit they have made. The thing is, the only way they can realise that profit is if they sell their home which, let's face it, most people would be fairly reluctant to do.

For many people, owning their own home will still be incredibly important and, if you do the maths and are prepared to compromise in locality, it can still make great financial sense.

However, I do believe the tide is changing, particularly as the size of a mortgage in some suburbs and capital cities increases to seven figures. With a bit of creativity (and the courage to swim against the tide), you may find that home ownership simply isn't the right fit for you, allowing you to look for bricks and mortar in investments rather than the home you live in.

IF YOU'VE LISTED THE PROS AND CONS AND DECIDED SOME TYPE OF PROPERTY OWNERSHIP (WHETHER IT'S YOUR HOME OR AN INVESTMENT) IS FOR YOU, HERE ARE MY TIPS TO MAKE SURE IT'S A SAFER INVESTMENT.

Borrow at 6% minimum. Your first step when purchasing a house should be working out what you can afford – and it's not at the current interest rates, no matter what the advertisers tell you. Determine what you can borrow at the very minimum at 6%. And don't cheat! Because when you sit down and work out the amount you can borrow at current interest rates you might realise that suddenly your dream house is a reality because the bank will lend you almost a million quid. But trust me when I say that your fairy tale will become a nightmare when interest rates start to move. Notice I said 'when' and not 'if'. That's why it's so important to decide your limit, determine not to budge from it and then, and only then, to start looking.

Buy with your head not with your heart. I understand that some people want a house to speak to them and I also understand that sometimes you can walk into a house and it just doesn't feel right. The problem happens when you become so attached to a house that you simply must have it and nothing, not even the fact that it's outside your budgeted price range, will stop you from making your dream a reality. My suggestion is to make a list of things you can't live without and then strike off at least 50% of them because, let's be honest, they're just wishes, not needs. Then, when you find the house that matches your list don't decide it's fate and you have to have it no matter what! Do your research, determine if it's within your budget and if it's not, move on. And if it's an investment property, there shouldn't be any emotion involved! In more cases than not, I haven't set foot into the investment properties I've purchased.

Use a buyer's agent. If you suspect that on auction day you'll be swept away by the emotion of the house you want – which ticks every box on your checklist and you know the bank will lend you more, so to hell with it – then stay away! Or if you know you'll give in to the notion that you've been looking long enough, you deserve it, you only live once (even the banks are telling you not to miss out), so you just keep pushing above your maximum budget until you're the excited owner, then again – stay away! Or maybe you're the competitive type and you just know that you'll keep bidding until you've won, dammit – again, stay away! Instead, send a representative, whether it be a buyer's agent, a trusted friend or a family member and insist that they do not go above your maximum limit. To not even call you to ask if it's OK to up your limit and to refuse to take your call until the auction is over.

Use a reputable estate agent and do your research. Good estate agents know their areas and know their valuations. You absolutely need to do your research too, though. Ask questions, find a great advisor and use property websites to check stats. If you're buying an investment property and aren't sure where you should buy, good estate agents can be a great source to help you choose unemotionally where to invest. And remember, there's no need to buy. You might date a few before you find one that is right for you.

Marketers will always appeal to your emotions and buying a home or investment property is probably one of the most emotional – and certainly the most expensive – decisions you'll ever make. That's why it's so important to try and remove as much of the emotion from the decision as possible. That way your head is ruling the decision and your heart can make an appearance only when the head has given the green light.

After all, there will be a whole lot more long-term damaging emotions to contend with if interest rates move upwards. Or if you take a punt on the area that your best mate's gardener told you is the next hot market mover, than the short-term pain of missing out.

So is home ownership right for you, or should you consider another way of investing in property instead? Write your own list of pros and cons, do the maths and then, and only then, start looking.

"SUCCESSFUL INVESTING TAKES TIME, DISCIPLINE AND PATIENCE. NO MATTER HOW GREAT THE TALENT OR EFFORT, SOME THINGS JUST TAKE TIME: YOU CAN'T PRODUCE A BABY IN ONE MONTH BY GETTING NINE WOMEN PREGNANT."
WARREN BUFFETT

what's the deal with shares?

I t's a fairly accepted truth that a lot of people are far more comfortable with property than they are with shares. Despite most of us having at least some exposure to the share market via our pension funds.

Perhaps it's because we're not comfortable with the short-term volatility of shares, despite them generally performing well long term. Maybe it's because we can touch our properties and drive past them, whereas we don't feel like we have the same level of control with shares. Or perhaps it's because we don't understand the first thing about dividends, AGMs and financial statements.

The thing is, smart investors will always try to have some understanding of where their money is being invested. They'll also try to have a diversified portfolio so that if one type of investment drops they're not all in.

If you're concerned the stock market is really just a legalised form of betting and you don't know where to start – but you know you should start somewhere – then read on.

TO HELP ENSURE YOUR SHARE MARKET INVESTMENT IS A WORTHWHILE ONE, HERE IS A HANDY CHEAT SHEET TO GET YOU STARTED.

In a nutshell, how should you approach buying shares? Cautiously, like you'd approach a horse. Because throwing a wad of money at a hot tip from your best mate's hairdresser (who made a ton of money on the stock market back in the day and now just gardens for fun) is essentially a bet. Instead, how you should approach buying shares is the same way you'd approach anything new. Do your research, ask for advice, read up on it, watch videos and then slowly dip your toe in.

How do you pick a decent stock? Like anything, there are people espousing their magic formulas and get-rich-quick schemes – but if there was an easy solution, we'd all be millionaires. Instead, a simple approach is to invest in what you know. For example, I'm an accountant and when the Cloud accounting solution Xero floated a couple of years ago and I saw the potential of both the product and the marketing plan, it made sense to invest. It's about soaking up as much information as you can and understanding current and upcoming trends. A current trend is the ageing population in the UK, so an industry that will service baby boomers' needs as they age may be worth a look at.

How do you make money from shares? You make money from shares through dividends, generally a twice-yearly amount that is paid to shareholders from the company's earnings. You can also make money from shares when you sell them, if your share price is higher than when you bought them. A wise stockbroker once told me that it's not a profit until it's in your bank, meaning your shares might be going up – but until you sell them and realise that gain, they can just as easily go down.

How can you lose money on shares? Easily! The share price can drop from poor management, poor public sentiment, lost faith in the CEO or a government policy change. Volks-wagen famously lost value when the emissions scandal broke in 2015.

Are there 'safe' shares to buy? Safer shares are generally called blue chip shares. Meaning they're shares in a large, well-established and financially sound company that has operated for many years. The major banks are generally thought of as blue chip shares – and historically you'd make more from buying bank shares than having your money in their accounts. It also means that when they release their profit figures, instead of fuming you'll be smiling because you'll benefit from that profit through dividends and increased share prices.

How long can you expect to have your money in shares before you start to make money? If I had a crystal ball that could answer that question, I'd be rich myself! You can be lucky and pop your money into shares and they go up next week, or you can be unlucky and they go down. There is an old adage that it's about time in the market rather than timing the market, so I would generally want to have a much longer mindset than twelve months.

Can you still bag a bargain? If I'm lusting after a pair of shoes I'll often wait for them to be on sale. But some shoes are so good that I'm happy to pay a bit more. Shoes you buy while holidaying in Bali are generally only worth the £1 you pay for them, as they fall apart in a couple of wears. Shares are no different. If your aim is to hold your shares for the long term, and you're buying them up gradually over a decade, then the fluctuations should even out. But if you're chasing the penny dreadfuls in the hope of bagging a bargain, you might simply be kissing a whole lot of frogs. That's because cheap shares don't always represent good value for money.

How much should I invest? If I want to start running I'm not going to sign up immediately for a marathon. Instead I might start with 10km, then a half-marathon and build my way up. It's the same with shares. Start with an amount of money you're comfortable with and, just as importantly, an amount of money where if it falls in value you won't lose any sleep.

How do you make sense of company reports? Often company reports are sleep-inducing tomes full of way too much jargon. Instead of reading the whole thing cover to cover you might start with the Chairman's address so you can get a feel for whether the person at the top can explain clearly and succinctly what's going on. Next, head straight to the numbers pages – the Profit and Loss, Balance Sheet and Cashflow Statements. Some key numbers to look at are Earnings, Sales and Equity, all of which you'd prefer to see higher than the year before. You might also take a look at Debt and make sure it's lower or about the same as the year before and lower than the company's assets.

How do you understand industry terminology? The good news is you don't need a financial planning or accounting degree, but you do need to have a basic understanding of a company's financials. There is everything from online courses and newspaper investment guides to books, as well as a wealth of information available via free newsletters and our good friend Google. The industry terminology you might want to start with includes EBIT (earnings before interest and taxes), price-to-earnings ratio, price-to-sales ratio, return-on-equity, earnings growth and debt-to-asset ratio. Again, it's not about knowing how to prepare a set of company accounts, it's about how to comprehend a few critical pages.

Do you need an advisor and how do you find a good one? If you really don't have the time or inclination then a good advisor is essential. Of course, the most important thing is not to abdicate all care and responsibility to your advisor, but to stay informed and continue keeping an eye on things yourself.

What are some alternatives? ETFs (exchange traded funds). If you're not comfortable choosing your own shares (and let's be honest, stock selection can be fraught with danger, even if you know what you're doing), then Index Funds can be a great alternative. An Index Fund will track the market index (for example, the top 100 UK shares) rather than try to time investing in individual shares. They're one of Warren Buffett's hot tips for smaller investors. Buffett's advice for small investors is to put their dough into index-tracking funds because of their broad diversification and low costs. 'A very low-cost index is going to beat a majority of the amateur-managed money or professionally managed money,' he says.

Unlike the property market, where we don't see the daily fluctuations in price values and it's not so easy to liquify our funds, the stock market can be an emotional rollercoaster.

The important thing is to make a plan, educate yourself, stay informed and have discipline around buying and selling. The same is true as it is for any type of investing – don't bet the house on your neighbour's hot stock tips – and there's no such thing as stupid questions.

"When we own portions of outstanding businesses with outstanding managements, our favourite holding period is forever."
Warren Buffett

sexuall
transmitted
debt

"A WOMAN'S BEST PROTECTION IS A LITTLE
MONEY OF HER OWN." CLARE BOOTHE LUCE

sexually transmitted debt

When you're in the first bloom of romance, let's face it, you don't want to be thinking about everything that could possibly go wrong with your budding relationship.

Yet at school, in sex education classes and in magazines we're urged to do just that. To protect ourselves from STDs (sexually transmitted diseases). We're encouraged to take off our rose-coloured glasses when it comes to new partners, to get tested and use protection.

Which is incredibly sensible advice and, when it comes to sex, generally we all comply. When it comes to potential partners and our finances, however, it's another story entirely.

Without meaning to we can find ourselves behaving recklessly and exposing ourselves to something that is just as damaging, and certainly as long-lasting, as any physical STD.

We risk catching an STD (sexually transmitted debt).

Now, you may be thinking that as you don't have any money you can't possibly receive an STD. Or perhaps you're thinking your partner knows what they're doing when it comes to your finances (and you don't), so you feel safe.

Let me encourage you to think again.

Every month I meet with many men and women who are currently struggling with an STD they received from a once-loving partner.

In one case the partner was a high-flying executive who took a few risks, drained the savings and then fled overseas, leaving his wife liable for the mountain of debts he left behind. In another case the partner was a tradesman and hid from his partner the fact that he hadn't lodged a tax return for almost a decade. When he eventually did, the debt was tens of thousands of dollars and the couple's house had to be sold to pay it. In yet another instance the wife had a secret gambling addiction and didn't pay bills or taxes. She eventually drained the bank accounts and the husband was left with enormous business and personal debts.

In every single one of these real-life examples, one party was left devastated and with a nasty case of STD.

But let's ignore the STD for a moment. Research tells us again and again that money is the number one thing couples fight about. The fighting takes place on average two to three times a month.

Wouldn't it be nice to side-step that argument?

TO AVOID BOTH THE QUARRELS AND THE POTENTIAL STD, HOW DO YOU START OFF ON THE RIGHT FINANCIAL FOOT IN A RELATIONSHIP AND AVOID BEING A STATISTIC?

1 **Use protection.** Author Clare Booth Luce once said: 'A woman's best protection is a little money of her own' – and I believe this is absolutely true in any relationship. For both partners. Sure, you might decide to have joint bank accounts, but retaining independence by always having some money in your own account is simply financially smart. It's also important to protect whatever assets you have, regardless of how small they currently are, including all of your employment income. Protection means not opening joint bank

accounts, joint credit cards, co-signing loans, moving in together, signing up to phone plans or other contracts until you've moved through Steps 2, 3, 4 and 5.

2 Talk about it. Before you get serious – and definitely before you start to share any sort of financial products, including bank accounts, credit cards, phone/internet, rental agreements and more – make sure you have a conversation about money. This includes who owns what, who owes what, what taxes are outstanding and what you hope to achieve with your finances. I'm also a huge advocate of doing the Goals, Values and Money Mindfulness exercises together. Now, I appreciate there is a giant ick factor associated with talking about money, but sometimes you simply have to put on your big-girl/boy pants and have the conversation. This means there should be fewer surprises down the track and, if there are any financial skeletons, you can both make a plan to deal with them early on. I'm not suggesting you won't move forward as a couple just because one of you has credit card debt, but it's important to understand what you're committing to before you take the step of joining your lives together – as well as understanding what your money values are. Misaligned money values are one of the biggest issues in relationships, and I'm a firm believer that if this was talked about earlier you could deal with it together and become closer as a result. Or, if there's enormous misalignment, perhaps choose to end the relationship. The big word here is choice.

3 Insist on transparency. While talking is a great first step, it's really important to see what's going on with your own eyes. After all, talk can be cheap, right? Make it hard for each other to financially cheat by deciding to share with each other what you have and what you owe. I'm talking eyeballs on bank statements. I don't necessarily advocate knowing each other's passwords and logins, particularly early in a relationship, as that removes some of your safety net. However, I am a fan of having a weekly, fortnightly or monthly chat around how you're going financially, where you either bring up your financial balances on a computer or bring along your bank statements. One way to be financially transparent without any risk is to use a spending tracker (there are some listed at the end of the book) where you can see each other's information, but can't access the funds. Now, this isn't so you can audit each other's spending – God knows, I don't need my husband to understand exactly how much money I spend on shoes! However, what he does need to understand is that I'm not in financial strife because of my spending patterns and I'm not putting what we're working towards at risk.

4 **Understand the risks.** The relationship is getting serious and you're talking about moving in together. In your mind, it's a 'try before you buy' arrangement where you're thinking that this could be the one, but you're not quite ready for marriage, kids and a commitment just yet. The problem is, sometimes you've already made the financial commitment of 'marriage' by moving in together without you being aware of the implications. There are time periods that are important to understand for de facto relationships and it can be worthwhile seeking legal advice if you do have assets

of your own before you take the step of moving in. It's the unsexy side of living together, but if you have a business, earn decent money or come into the relationship with assets, then it makes sense to protect what you have.

5 **Always seek professional advice.** Before you take the giant step of joining funds, moving in together, applying for loans or signing documents, always seek professional advice. It's so important to understand the worst-case scenario or to be made aware of the implications of what you're signing. For example, if you and your partner move in together and both your names are on the lease, but your partner leaves and you can't afford to pay, the landlord won't necessarily chase you both for the money. He'll chase the easiest one to locate and the one that is earning an income. The same goes for signing documents. You may be told it's not a big deal to guarantee a loan or become a company director for a business, but the ramifications if your partner can't pay, or the company is late lodging or paying its debts, can be life-changing. And ignorance, or the argument that you were too trusting or didn't understand what you were signing, is simply not an excuse that will get you out of the debt.

Sex, money and relationships. Often we focus entirely on the sexual side of a relationship because it can be the most fun, but it's money issues that can cause the most lasting damage.

By choosing to be purposeful about money, couples can not only avoid STDs but can create strong relationships where money isn't something dirty or awkward, but is just another thing that is talked about.

"This would be a much better world if more married couples were as deeply in love as they are in debt."
Earl Wilson

"I FOUND THAT EVERY SINGLE SUCCESSFUL PERSON I'VE EVER SPOKEN TO HAD A TURNING POINT AND THE TURNING POINT WAS WHERE THEY MADE A CLEAR, SPECIFIC, UNEQUIVOCAL DECISION THAT THEY WERE NOT GOING TO LIVE LIKE THIS ANYMORE. SOME PEOPLE MAKE THAT DECISION AT 15 AND SOME PEOPLE MAKE IT AT 50 AND MOST NEVER MAKE IT AT ALL."
BRIAN TRACY

how you can f*ck up your finances at any age

Most of us accept we'll make mistakes in life. Our dilemma when it comes to money mistakes is that there's an ick factor associated with talking about money. We feel ashamed if we don't have it together financially. Which means we don't fess up.

Which as you've figured out by now, means we don't learn from each other's financial f*ck-ups.

The problem is, if we want to avoid making the same money mistakes we kind of need to know how we're stuffing up.

Which is hard to do if no one's talking.

HERE'S MY GUIDE UNTIL WE START SHARING. THE KEY MONEY MISTAKES YOU NEED TO LOOK OUT FOR AND HOW CAN YOU AVOID THEM AT EACH LIFE STAGE.

University and college students. With easy credit and student loans it can be tempting to defer a large portion of student life. Yes, it's incredibly tough to work two or three jobs and study, but it's far better to walk away from university with only a student debt rather than a stack of other debts you also need to pay back. If you're financially struggling, maybe consider working full-time and studying part-time, or working for a year, building up funds and then heading back to study with more time and more money.

First job (your twenties). You've decided to enjoy your first year of work and get serious about saving at the end of twelve months. Before you know it, three years have passed and you have nothing to show for all your hard work. Your friend, meanwhile, has racked up some nasty credit card debt trying to keep up with the group, while another has a large loan for a new car they just had to have. Sure, you want to enjoy life, but get into the habit from the moment you start working of automatically transferring a percentage of your wage to a savings account you can't access. It's setting up good financial habits and taking advantage of compound interest at a time when you potentially have very few large regular expenses. Which might also mean being kind to your future self by popping a little extra each pay rise into a pension.

Singles. The danger for singles is that they often financially press pause until they meet a partner. If you're single you need to reject the money message that a man (or woman) is a financial plan and start building assets yourself. Without a partner to help with the cost of home-ownership and sharing the bills, you might need to consider other options or become more flexible. This might include taking in a lodger, or buying an investment property in your own name, then renting instead of buying your own home. The most important thing is deciding to become the hero of your own story and save yourself financially.

Coupling. With money being the number one thing couples fight about it's important to get on the same financial page early on. This means talking about money, working out your shared goals, insisting on transparency and understanding the financial ramifications of how you're getting together.

Thirties and forties. For many of us these are our peak earning years and it's important, whether you're single, a couple, a DINK (dual income, no kids) or have kids to make sure you're financially smart. This means not increasing your spending with every pay rise. Instead, make sure you limit the size of the spending bowl by siphoning a chunk of your pay rise into your savings bowl, or using it to pay down debt or save for retirement.

DINKs. Couples who are childfree, and this includes myself, are generally in a unique position financially. We don't have the additional financial burden of children such as food, childcare or school fees and generally have higher discretionary incomes. The trick is to ensure you are still enjoying life but also understand what your goals, values and priorities are when it comes to money so you're tempted to save and not just spend. These goals might include planned sabbaticals, extended trips away, helping nieces and nephews or starting a charity. There is very little excuse for most DINKs not to be accumulating serious assets, so sort yourself out mentally, then financially, and start building.

Families. We might think we won't try to keep up with the Joneses, but when your friend's child is going to a private school, has a new bike and all the latest gadgets and your child starts asking for them too, are you going to fall into the guilt trap? It's important to understand that getting yourself into trouble financially is not helpful for your family. It's also crucial not to become financially stressed and put pressure on your family relationships by overextending yourself – whether that's with the size of your mortgage, your choice of school or any number of things parents feel they should be doing. Work out what you value, what the goals are for your family, set out a financial plan to get there, work out your bowls, automate and then track. I'm a huge fan of bringing your kids into these conversations so they can be aware that there isn't a money tree in the backyard and they can start to become financially literate at an early age.

Consciously uncoupling. It's a fact of life that many couples will split. In protracted and messy settlement disputes, the only ones who win are the lawyers. It's incredibly important to receive great advice as soon as you can so you know what you should and shouldn't be doing, but whenever possible agreeing on a fair and equitable split early on means you can start again with more dollars in your pocket. It's also important not to let emotion get the better of you – which is much easier said than done. For example, don't do what I did and give the entire pot to charity so you start with a 'clean slate'. Which was an emotional reaction to him saying I wouldn't make it on my own. But at the end of the day it was just plain dumb. It's all about looking after yourself financially for the long term. If it sounds like a Utopian ideal to remove the emotion and think rationally, make sure you have someone on your side that can act as a sounding board so you're not gut-reacting in a way that's financially harmful to you.

Other mistakes to avoid at all life stages? The big one I see all too often is people not adequately insuring their assets. My rule of thumb is that if you can't afford the insurance, you can't afford the asset. Simple. Oh – and you're an asset too, so make sure you at least have life insurance and income protection insurance.

"WHO RUNS THE WORLD?
GIRLS." BEYONCÉ

girlboss like you mean it

T his chapter is intentionally and strategically aimed at the ladies. Of course, blokes, you're welcome to hang around as well.

Because starting a business can be a great way of adding to your wealth and increasing your income whether you're a man or a woman. Personally, I've always bet on myself and owning three businesses is a big part of my wealth creation and financial plan.

But there's a particular financial reason why I'm lecturing the gals here.

Internationally, there is a lot of talk about gender parity, but often the conversation has centred around females in the workforce and the boardroom. What I find interesting is the difference in pay that exists in one area where women should be on an equal footing with men. In business.

A 2015 Startup Muster survey discovered the percentage of start-ups founded by females had risen from one in six in 2011 to one in four in 2014. While the Australian Bureau of Statistics (ABS) reported in that same year that 34% of businesses operators were women. The stats are similar in the UK and the US.

This represents an increase in business ownership by females of more than 46% in the last twenty years.

So, it's fairly clear that women are starting businesses faster than ever. What concerns me, however, is that we're generally not doing it as profitably as our male counterparts.

Which is why this chapter is designed as a wake-up call to 'fempreneurs' or women who are thinking of starting a business.

A 2015 ABS study in Australia reported that in 2012 women were earning on average $423 per week compared with $890 for men for an unincorporated business, and $998 as compared to $1,451 per week for an incorporated business. While female business owners were also likely to have less money per week from all sources than their male counterparts and other employed women. Similar research mirrored these findings in the US and the UK.

It's also clear from research and reports that women who run their own businesses are neglecting to pay into pensions and other benefits for themselves. Which means, sure, women might be starting businesses at a faster rate, but at what cost?

Now can you see why I'm talking to you, ladies?

Now, I'm all for the rise of the female entrepreneur. After all, I am one.

But I'm for the rise of the fempreneur who refuses to use the word 'just' when describing their business. Who is determined to make their business, whether it's a two-day-a-week enterprise or a global business, the most successful one it can be.

Which also means the most profitable one.

After all, you don't need to avoid money to do good. In fact, wanting to make a profit can mean you effect more social good, as Audette Exel from Adara Group and many other incredible female entrepreneurs have shown. The problem arises because of the money messages women carry around with them, the guilt they feel when it comes to wanting to make money in their businesses, their desire to do good rather than make cash.

The money side of business, for many female business owners, just feels icky.

So how do female business owners begin to close the gap? How do we not simply start a business, but manage to run one that is just as profitable and successful as those of our male counterparts?

MY ALL-TIME BUSINESS CRUSH, JIM COLLINS, IN HIS BOOK *GOOD TO GREAT*, RESEARCHED WHY SOME BUSINESSES FLOUNDER AND OTHERS GO ON TO BECOME GREAT. THE PROBLEM IS THE RESEARCHED COMPANIES WERE ALMOST ENTIRELY MALE-RUN, WITH MALE CEOS OR BOARDS. WHICH IS WHY I BELIEVE, FOR WOMEN, IT COMES DOWN TO ACCEPTING MY REVISED VERSION OF COLLINS' 'HEDGEHOG CONCEPT', WHICH INVOLVES THREE EQUALLY IMPORTANT PARTS.

1 **Developing a passion for business.** The first part of Collins' theory involves developing passion for what you're doing. In my experience, most women who start a business do so based on passion, so they already have that in spades. Instead, women need to develop a passion for business. Often this means putting on your big-girl pants and choosing to understand the numbers side of your business. This includes embracing business basics such as budgets, business plans, costs, capacity, the psychology of pricing, critical numbers and more. Many women who have started a business once worked in the corporate world where they dealt with all these

things on a daily basis, so it's not the fact that you can't. Often, it's the fact that this side of business doesn't necessarily light you up. It's not what drives you.

If you're like many women, you're not motivated by the financial side of business. Hopefully, by reading this book you've come to understand that your goals are worth your business creating a sustainable profit. And here's the secret when it comes to business. You don't need to become an accountant – you just need to understand the numbers that are critical to your business and the activity that will help you achieve the results you want.

2 **Being the best in the world at what you do.** Now, I know many male business owners who truly believe they're the best in the world at what they do. In fact, I know many men who truly believe they're the best in the world at many things. After all, I'm married to a bald, pasty man who believes he's Daniel Craig. That's because men have something many female business owners lack – confidence.

Now, before you start to feel uncomfortable, before you start to feel that this is just not you: stop. The point isn't to be the best in the world, but rather to be the best version of yourself doing that thing in your business that you do. In other words, not being a carbon copy of something or someone you think you should be, but bringing the best version of you to the business. It's about authenticity, showing up for your tribe and developing a product or service that others can't replicate because it has your secret sauce.

As a boutique accountant, can I compete with large firms

when it comes to expertise? Probably not. But I can compete with them – and even be the best in the world – by being a financial advisor using my own voice, my own skills and my unique way of doing it. Don't believe me? I was recently invited into a top-tier accounting firm to talk to seventy women about their finances. Why invite a boutique financial advisor? Because I can cut through to their women in a unique way that they can't. I've strategically taken a path that means I'm becoming known for being one of the best in the world (yes, it hurts to write that sentence because, like you, I'm still on my way to believing it) at helping women with their finances.

3 **Figuring out what drives your economic engine.** Yes, it sounds blokey, but it's hard to find a better description. That's because there are some women (and men) who are calling their hobby a business, whereas they'd be much better off going and getting a job because what they're doing and what they're able or willing to price it for just isn't viable. Figuring out what drives your economic engine is all about understanding your numbers, understanding where your profit pools are and making smart decisions about what you're going to spend your time and business doing.

That's because you may love tea cosies, you may be passionate about them and about your business, you may be the best in the world at making them and your creations could light up Instagram – but if you can't sell them for a high enough price, or make them efficiently enough, or scale to such a point that your business is worthwhile, then you probably shouldn't be starting a business selling tea cosies. Understanding where your profit pools are can turn your business from a ho-hum business or hobby into a standout one.

There are more and more people and organisations championing the rise of the fempreneur and I think that's a great thing. I'm also all for people adding revenue streams so that they're increasing their money coming in and, ultimately, their wealth.

But at the end of the day, it should be about more than just females starting businesses. Instead, it should be about more women committed to understanding how to run successful businesses, who are paying into their pension, building wealth and, through their influence, truly creating a difference.

After all, when it comes to parity in the business world, it really is up to us.

Want to know more about running a great business? Head to the 'Work With Us' section at the back of the book and find out how you can learn to create and run an amazing, sustainable, profitable business. Or order a copy of my book for women in business (or thinking of starting a business), *More Money for Shoes*.

"THE WAY YOU TELL YOUR STORY TO
YOURSELF MATTERS." AMY CUDDY

celebrating vs rewards

W e're not dogs, although many of us behave as if we are. Particularly when it comes to doing a good job and feeling we should be rewarded. I mean, all that's missing is 'good girl/boy' and a pat on the head.

Don't pretend you haven't done it.

You reached the end of a tough year/quarter/month/week/day and you decided you deserved some sort of gift, treat or reward for seeing it through. Perhaps the reward was the result of something you'd recovered from, perhaps it was a new business you'd launched, or perhaps it was a new role or promotion you landed.

The end result was you deciding you deserved a reward.

Good dog.

Your reward may have been a Prada handbag, an overseas trip, a weekly shopping indulgence or a new toy. The bottom line is you chose to spend some hard-earned cash on yourself for a job well done.

I'm not going to suggest that rewarding our effort is a bad thing. I think it's important to celebrate milestones. But I also believe it's necessary to understand the true cost of the pat on the back you're giving yourself.

Because every decision we make has an opportunity cost.

You might think of it as simply acknowledging that a boozy night out brings the consequence of a morning lost nursing a hangover. It doesn't mean you regret having a night out celebrating with friends, but if you missed an important meeting the next morning, you might have changed your behaviour. Or at least limited your drinks and left a few hours earlier.

The same is true for your finances.

If you're going to give yourself a reward, you need to understand and acknowledge the unintended consequences.

It's a big step towards becoming a conscious consumer and making informed choices.

Because the £100 you're splashing on yourself every week for surviving Hump Day might seem like a good idea – but that's £5,200 you're spending annually for surviving Wednesday.

Really?

Or the £5,000 you splashed out on the Prada handbag as a reward for receiving a pay rise, which is now sitting on your credit card, may end up costing you more than your incrementally increased wage.

IF WE ACKNOWLEDGE THAT WE NEED TO CELEBRATE, THAT WE WANT TO ACKNOWLEDGE MILESTONES, WHAT DO WE NEED TO BE AWARE OF IF WE'RE TREATING OURSELVES?

✱ Rewarding yourself with cash you've saved is fine, but it's problematic if you pop the reward onto a credit card and only repay the minimum amount. Because the £5,000 present you bought yourself may cost you an unexpected £12,181 in interest and you'll still have the debt some thirty-three years later. Even if you knuckle down and pay the amount off over two years, you'll still pay an extra £902 in interest on an average card. Which, for a reward that will either simply be a memory or will depreciate in value, doesn't really make great financial sense.

✳ Even worse is the opportunity cost of what you could have saved during the time you were making those credit card repayments. If you transferred the minimum repayments you made on the credit card into a bank account earning 2% interest you'd have saved £24,090 over thirty-three years or £6,019 on the minimum repayments made in two years. Now, a bank account with almost £25,000 versus a credit card with a nil balance and nothing to show for it decades later seems like a no-brainer to me.

✳ Of course, you might thumb your nose at a 2% interest rate and look for a higher return, meaning your opportunity cost might soar too. Instead of buying something tangible you might reward yourself with an investment. Whether you bought the bank by purchasing bank shares rather than depositing your money in an account, purchased an index fund, or popped your money into an ethical fund, you could potentially see your opportunity cost double. Or you might reward yourself with only half the amount, invest the balance and still be able to enjoy a treat while looking after your future self. It's important to understand your risk profile and your longer-term goals before making an investment, but it's certainly worth considering an alternative to cash in the bank.

✳ While you might think that if you have cash sitting in a bank account you can do what you want, it's important to understand what your goals, priorities and values are when it comes to money. If your goal is to start a business next year and you've decided you need a buffer of £10,000 to do it (which you have sitting in a bank account), grabbing half to reward yourself is really only hurting you and delaying your dreams. This is when it's time to look at yourself honestly and ask if your slightly longer-term goal is worth more than your short-term gratification. Which might mean trading the Prada bag for a much cheaper quarterly celebratory spa session – which means your savings are intact and your business can start on schedule.

You might have decided by now that I'm the fun police – and shouldn't we have some fun and enjoy life? Aren't we supposed to celebrate achievements? Absof*ckinglutely.

But not at the expense of your financial goals. Not at the expense of the life you're designing for yourself.

Rod Soper, my co-founder at Thinkers.inq, and I love celebrating. We love treats, but we also know we need to be really sensible because we're building a business together and it doesn't have a lot of spare cash. But we wanted a motivator. We wanted a treat. So we came up with a plan where every time we achieved certain strategic and key financial milestones in our business we would open a bottle of champagne together. And the celebratory bottle became better and pricier the bigger the milestones we hit.

Did we both receive a giddy high as we popped that champagne? Absolutely. Did we feel rewarded? Absolutely. Did the bottles of champagne ever cost more than £100? Absolutely not.

That's because it's about spending what you can afford. Building your celebrations into your financial plan and enjoying them, knowing they're not going to financially derail you.

If you need a treat every week to get over Hump Day, make it something less than £20. Or if you want it to be worth £100 then make sure it's in your Everyday Account and ask yourself what you're prepared to go without in order to treat yourself.

That way you're making conscious financial choices that aren't going to f*ck your finances.

Advertisers want us to believe 'we're worth it' and we should be spending money on ourselves and enjoying today. I'm certainly not suggesting that you're not worth it and that you never should enjoy yourself.

For me, the reward is almost always shoes, day spas or a glass of champagne.

What is important is to understand the real cost of rewarding yourself. To understand your behaviour and question if you need a reward as regularly as you're treating yourself. To factor those treats and rewards into either your Holiday Account or your Everyday Account and enjoy the experience fully rather than feeling guilt-ridden if you've decided to go for it.

Or to applaud yourself for your restraint if you've decided not to. Because you're worth it.

"Buy Less. Choose Well."
Vivienne Westwood

"WE NEED MUCH LESS THAN WE
THINK WE NEED." MAYA ANGELOU

you are not what you have

L et me tell you a bit about me. You already know more than most people, but here are a few more fun facts.

I'm a Western Suburbs 'bogan', as they say in Australia. Born at Blacktown Hospital. Grew up in Penrith and moved house at least seven times before I hit sixteen. Which is less than some, but more than most. Public primary school, public high school for a couple of years, and then private school because I was lazy. There's no other word for it. Bullied for years at school. Spent most of my life trying not to be a victim and in the process behaved just like one. I still can't say the word comfortably, so let's just say I'm a statistic: one of the one in four. Recovered anorexic/bulimic. Once divorced. Twice married. Entrepreneur. Accountant. Financial Advisor. CEO. Author. Writer. Strife. Purposely child-free. Introvert. Socially awkward.

I've spent my life running away from labels like so many of those above. I also tried for a long time to fill my life with stuff and status, hoping it would wipe away some of my perceived shame. Or I've fought with impostor-syndrome from some of the labels I've chosen for myself.

Fast forward to decades later and I'm proud of where I've come from and who I'm becoming. I'm proud of the labels in that paragraph because they're about where I've been, who I am and who I'm becoming. Would I choose them all? Hell, no. But for the most part, I accept them because I'm comfortable with the woman I want to be.

Not every day, but most.

And I know, deep within me, that the woman I want to be has absolutely nothing to do with what I have.

In fact, my dirty little secret is that my husband and I truly know we could sell up tomorrow and move into the little rental house we first moved into together a decade ago. That's because I know my happiness, my sense of self and my sense of fulfilment doesn't come from what I have.

It comes from who I am.

Which is an incredibly important distinction to make.

Today, too many people are filling their lives with stuff and experiences because they figure that what they have is who they are. Which is why we have so many fake posts and falseness filling our social media feeds because people are trying to show a life that isn't really theirs, that they're paying for on credit, to draw 'likes' from people they've never met yet are trying desperately to impress.

Which must be incredibly bloody exhausting.

I mean, enough already. Let's start figuring out who we want to be, not what we want to have (or for people to think we have).

Which seems counterintuitive. I mean, isn't this a book about unf*cking your finances and building financial resilience and financial wellness? Doesn't that mean you kind of need to want to have savings and investments and stuff?

Yes, yes. I know. But stick with me. Because designing the life we want means figuring out who we want to be. What legacy we want to leave to the world. What our purpose is. That's when we start to realise that money is a tool that, if used correctly, will help us live our best life. Rather than scheming, plotting and getting ourselves into f*ckloads of debt because we have a twisted notion that life is about accumulating stuff.

I mean, we just need to stop it.

I believe if you embrace the concepts in this book you'll start to realise you are not what you have. You'll start to question decisions you've made such as where you live, what you're doing, what you have and what you owe. Hopefully you'll start to make some new great decisions which fit in with the life you're designing.

Which means you can kick the nonsense concept of 'you are what you have' out of your head completely.

If I'm ever tempted to think that way I think of my 'why', my personal mission and who I want to be. Which is all about creating transformational change and moving people from and to.

If that doesn't work I think about my grandparents.

I don't know about yours, but my grandparents had gumption. I know it's not a word that's used very often today, but it perfectly describes so many of their generation.

I mean, they went through wars, they had family members who were taken prisoner or passed away during that war, they fled continents to escape invasion, they started businesses, they chose singledom over unhappy marriages.

That's all been part of my grandparents' experience anyway.

What I loved about my grandma, my grandpop and my nana is that they never had a lot of money (both sets of grandparents were on the age pension) – but they also never seemed to go without. I've been thinking of them a lot lately and it occurred to me that their experience with money and their inherent gumption is something we can learn from today.

Particularly if we're tempted to believe that we are what we have.

That's because my grandparents had so little. Yet they had so much. They lived full, complete, extraordinary lives. In all honesty they were, are and always will be, my heroes.

SO, IN CASE YOU DIDN'T HAVE GRANDPARENTS LIKE MINE, HERE ARE SOME FINANCIAL LESSONS I LEARNED FROM MY AMAZING SET THAT WILL HOPEFULLY HELP YOU IF YOU'RE STUCK IN THE TRAP OF NEEDING MORE AND MORE STUFF.

1 **Don't spend more than you earn.** My grandparents didn't grow up with credit, so they couldn't overspend. There was less choice and less opportunity to get into financial trouble, which meant they became incredibly creative because they were forced by necessity to do so. It also meant that my grandma and grandpop were somehow able to save money while on the pension and still go away in their caravan every winter. Yes, I know. Total financial rock stars.

2 **Always take home leftovers.** I distinctly remember the horror on a boyfriend's face the first time my grandparents wrapped up their second piece of fish at the RSL Club to take home for dinner that night. What I didn't explain to him was that they chose that dish purposefully so they would have leftovers. Restaurants often serve far more than we can eat, and if we're not choosing to share

dishes then where's the shame in asking to take home the leftovers? It's something we do at the pizza shop, so why not at Spice Temple? Think they won't? I can attest to the fact that they're very happy to do so – and the food tastes just as good the next day.

3 **Make your own soups, stews and other meals.** Yes, it means being organised, but cooking up a batch of food on a Sunday night is much cheaper than buying lunch every day. It's often healthier too, especially if you're comparing something like home-cooked bone broth to packet soup. My grandparents used to have a chest freezer where they would store cooked meals and leftovers so they would always have food for those days where they either didn't want to cook or had people turn up unexpectedly.

4 **Enjoy holidays and trips away sensibly.** My grandma and grandpop used to jump in their caravan and take off north to warmer climates for up to six months of the year. They'd travel in their caravan and stay at free sites or with friends and family. Too often when I talk with families they tell me if they take a cheap trip to Queensland they can't avoid taking their kids to the expensive theme parks, regardless of whether they can afford it or not. Really? Who's running the ship? It's about sitting your kids down and giving them choices. This might be Queensland beaches and no theme parks – or stay at home. Involve them in the conversation so they understand. Or if you absolutely must include the theme parks, then go away every second year and stay at home on the off year.

5 Shop vintage – or make your own. Throughout my teenage years and into my twenties I enjoyed many afternoons with my nana shopping in secondhand stores. Looking back, I didn't have many clothes so this was both a social outing and a necessity. Again, my nana was on the pension, but she absolutely loved clothes and jewellery and would hit the secondhand stores every week. Or she would make them herself.

6 Find a great tailor and a good cobbler. We are so used to throwing things away when they're slightly worn or out of date, but a great tailor and cobbler can save money as well as waste. It might be changing the shape of clothes, removing sleeves, reheeling a shoe or adding a rubber sole. Remaking or repairing an old classic might sound revolutionary, but it's what our grandparents did. OK, they probably did the mending themselves – but I can't sew to save my life so I've found a great tailor and shoe-repairer instead.

7 Grow your own. I remember the joy of walking into the backyard with my grandpop to pick vegetables from the garden for that day's meals. Whether it's growing your own vegetables in the backyard, growing some lettuce and herbs in a pot on your veranda or keeping a few chickens for eggs, there is enormous satisfaction and a substantial cost saving through harvesting your own food.

8 Play together. When we visited my grandparents we would eat dinner together and then play card games afterwards instead of watching TV. They couldn't afford satellite TV but we never felt we went without, as we would play card games for hours while munching on home-made goodies or white bread with jam.

9 **Share.** We have houses and sheds stacked with things we may only ever use occasionally. Instead of buying everything new, why not rent, share, borrow or swap instead. When I was growing up, my mum was in a babysitter's club where they swapped hours rather than paying for a babysitter. There are so many sites popping up now where you can rent, swap or share online from toys to clothes to tools and more.

10 **Be OK with who you are.** This might seem strange, but my grandparents trusted themselves. They knew who they were. Maybe it's because they'd been through so much, so young, that they didn't need to consume in order to have a sense of self. Now, I'm not suggesting that you go and find traumatic experiences to imbue yourself with a sense of self – but it is about starting to settle into who you are. Realising that who you are is enough and the latest bag won't add to that. No matter how pretty it is.

Thankfully we don't have to live through a world war or a worldwide Great Depression in order to work out that we are not what we have – but we can learn some incredible money and life lessons from those who did.

"Operation Self-
Esteem-Day
Fucking One."
Elizabeth Gilbert,
Eat, Pray, Love

just
stop it

"DOING WHAT YOU'VE BEEN DOING IS GOING TO GET YOU WHAT YOU'VE BEEN GETTING." SETH GODIN

CHAPTER TWENTY THREE

just stop it!

I love Karen James. She of the book *On Purpose* (add it to your reading list now, especially if you struggle with goals or have never thought about your personal mission) is a tough-talking, straight-shooting New Jersey girl and it was she who first told me about the 'Stop It' skit.

In the skit, Bob Newhart (you might remember him as the children's TV show Professor in *The Big Bang Theory*) is a psychologist who offers five-minute sessions at $5 a session (which is charged regardless of whether you take up one minute or five minutes.)

THE BEGINNING OF THE SKIT IS BELOW.

Katherine: I'm Katherine Bigmans. Janet Carlisle referred me.

Dr. Switzer: Oh, yes. You dream about being buried alive in a box.

Katherine: Yes, that's me. Should I lay down?

Dr. Switzer: No, we don't do that anymore. Just have a seat and let me tell you a bit about our billing. I charge five dollars for the first five minutes and then absolutely nothing after that. How does that sound?

Katherine: That sounds great. Too good to be true as a matter of fact.

Dr. Switzer: Well, I can almost guarantee you that our session won't last the full five minutes. Now, we don't do any insurance billing, so you would either have to pay in cash or by cheque.

Katherine: Wow. Okay.

Dr. Switzer: And I don't make change.

Katherine: All right.

Dr. Switzer: Go.

Katherine: Go?

Dr. Switzer: Tell me about the problem that you wish to address.

Katherine: Oh, okay. Well, I have this fear of being buried alive in a box. I just start thinking about being buried alive and I begin to panic.

Dr. Switzer: Has anyone ever tried to bury you alive in a box?

Katherine: No. No, but truly thinking about it does make my life horrible. I mean, I can't go through tunnels or be in an elevator or in a house, anything boxy.

Dr. Switzer: So, what you are saying is you are claustrophobic?

Katherine: Yes, yes, that's it.

Dr. Switzer: All right. Well, let's go, Katherine. I'm going to say two words to you right now. I want you to listen to them very, very carefully. Then I want you to take them out of the office with you and incorporate them into your life.

Katherine: Shall I write them down?

Dr. Switzer: No. If it makes you comfortable. It's just two words. We find most people can remember them.

Katherine: Okay.

Dr. Switzer: You ready?

Katherine: Yes.

Dr. Switzer: Okay. Here they are. Stop it!

Katherine: I'm sorry?

Dr. Switzer: Stop it!

Katherine: Stop it?

Dr. Switzer: Yes. S-T-O-P, new word, I-T.

Katherine: So, what are you saying?

Dr. Switzer: You know, it's funny, I say two simple words and I cannot tell you the amount of people who say exactly the same thing you are saying. I mean, you know, this is not Yiddish, Katherine. This is English. Stop it.

Katherine: So I should just stop it?

Dr. Switzer: There you go. I mean, you don't want to go through life being scared of being buried alive in a box, do you? I mean, that sounds frightening.

Katherine: It is.

Dr. Switzer: Then stop it.

Katherine: I can't. I mean it's–

Dr. Switzer: No, no, no. We don't go there. Just stop it.

Katherine: So, I should just stop being afraid of being buried alive in a box?

Dr. Switzer: You got it. Good girl.

Now, I know it's meant to be a funny skit and I'm aware that therapy is often a useful and necessary part of our lives. Trust me, I've spent years in it.

But part of the reason this skit is funny is because sometimes, especially when it comes to how you're behaving with your finances, you just need to call out your behaviour either aloud or in your head and yell, STOP IT!

When you pull your phone out on a Sunday night because

you're bored, you're not looking forward to the week, you start scrolling through your Instagram feed and next thing you know you're on your favourite store's site and about to click to buy, yell STOP IT!

When you meet friends for a boozy brunch and wander past the shops afterwards, which turns into a wander through the shops and into the changing room where your good intentions of the week threaten to come undone, yell STOP IT!

When your good friends move into a gorgeous apartment and you head back to your shitty place and decide you might not be able to afford a great pad but you could buy some flash wheels or new shoes, yell STOP IT!

It's the phrase that, if you keep saying it to yourself, and act on it, will save you from financially sabotaging yourself. Or even better, share it with your friends and family and give yourselves permission to use it on each other.

Besides, it's kind of fun.

Particularly when you yell it out loud in a change room with the shop assistant hovering outside.

It's all about taking back your power, and if you do this with friends and family you'll be ensuring you're all supporting each other to take back your power at the same time.

It's simple, silly (often the best things are), effective – and it's also kind of fun. Try it with me.

STOP IT!

"RING THE BELLS THAT STILL CAN RING.
FORGET YOUR PERFECT OFFERING.
THERE IS A CRACK IN EVERYTHING.
THAT'S HOW THE LIGHT GETS IN."
LEONARD COHEN

you're going to f*ck up . . . and that's ok!

Every year I decide to work on my fitness. Many years ago I used to play league netball, so my fitness was taken care of with an activity I really enjoyed. But it was functional fitness. My exercise regime was designed to help me perform better on the netball court.

Unfortunately age, my general klutziness and an ankle reconstruction wiped out any further netballing and I've been struggling with my fitness ever since.

I've tried rewards-based outcomes, DVDs and classes, gym memberships, signing up for fun runs, making up hashtags, buying outfits I want to wear to make it more fun, trying to con other people to work out with me and so much more. I've also tried working out intensively for a short time every day, working out three times a week, working out four times a week, working out for longer but less frequently, and many more versions.

The problem for me is that unless it's a team sport I generally don't enjoy exercise and, thanks to my dud ankle, most team sports are out. Which means I will find any and every excuse known to get out of exercising.

These excuses include, but are not limited to: I'm tired, I'm sick, my neck hurts, I'm too busy, I don't do mornings, it's dark, it's cold, it's hot, I don't feel like it, it's Monday, it's the end of a tough week, it's the start of a tough week, it's Wednesday, I'm tired, it's the first day of my period.

Do I need to keep going?

I also have the great excuse that I work bloody long hours and don't have many weekends when I'm not working at least some of the time. So, I act like my very own best friend by giving myself heaps of time off when it comes to working out.

Because I'm worth it.

Now, I'm sure many of you are nodding along because you do exactly the same thing. I'm also sure there are others who love exercising and are thinking I should just suck it up and do it.

It's OK, I think that too.

What's the solution to my exercising dilemma? I try different things, my husband writes me exercise programmes, I con others into working out with me, and I tell myself I have to work out three times a week.

Basically I suck it up.

I generally track well for six-week stints and then I fall off the wagon. I'm currently on my longest exercise failure yet, which has been three months of doing pretty much no exercise other than the occasional walk. But this weekend I've already planned to get back on track. To draw a line in the sand and start again.

It's no different with your finances.

You may never love this part of your life. You may always see it as a necessary evil. What you will enjoy, however, are the gains that becoming financially well will bring. Which means if you occasionally stuff up (and you will) you'll dust yourself off and keep going.

It would be easy for me to give up when it comes to exercising regularly. To work out that fitness and me are not a natural fit and, instead, to put my energy into reality TV or something far more enjoyable. However, I know that, ultimately, to enjoy life on the terms I want to, I need to sort myself out, get off the couch and move intentionally and frequently.

I know it's the same for many of you when it comes to money.

You may have tried many different types of budgets over the years and they all gradually fizzled out, along with your enthusiasm, after a few months. Or a few weeks. Or days. You may have tried different investment plans, different financial advisors, dabbled in the stock market or in property, and tried to understand your pension. You may have consolidated credit cards, cut up cards and vowed to have a zero balance every month. But when you look at your finances today, nothing's improved.

In fact, if it's anything like my fitness, you're probably in a worse position than when you started.

The problem is, as I realised, if you do nothing and choose failure then the only one who will suffer is you. Which is why I recommend taking a deep breath every time you have a financial blip or a financial f*ck-up and commit to trying again.

Trying again might involve speaking to a financial advisor, signing up to a course, trying a different tracking app or taking your credit cards out of your wallet. Trying again might be recommitting to all those great things you set up which were working for you, before you had that momentary relapse. Trying again might just mean trying and failing at the different concepts in this book until they eventually fall into place.

Which is why you need to acknowledge now that you're going to fail, that you're going to f*ck up – and that's OK.

It's like anything new.

If I decide to learn French this weekend I won't master it immediately. If I decide to cook my first soufflé it will probably deflate. If I decide to start riding a bike or run my first marathon I'm probably going to suffer cramps, injuries and setbacks.

Why should it be any different when it comes to having great finances?

I think that too often in life we're searching for the silver bullet. For the incredibly innovative thing that will pull us out of our financial pit. I don't think this mindset is limited to money, finances and the numbers, but it's something I see a lot of in this space.

The truth is there is no silver bullet. Instead there is trying, failing, trying something new, failing again, improving it, failing, tweaking it again, failing and eventually figuring out a system that works for you.

Some things simply don't come naturally or easily to us – and for some of you that's money and finances. Perhaps it's time for you to admit that and acknowledge that it's OK.

As you reach the end of this book, as you (hopefully) start to implement and try out the exercises, tools and tips throughout, I want you to acknowledge that it won't feel natural. That it won't be easy. That you'll fail.

What I want to encourage you to do is to persist. To build up resilience. To try again and again and again. And in that process of trying and failing, to eventually create amazing gradual improvements and habits that stick.

Which means, before you know it, you'll be financially well.

"OWNING OUR STORY CAN BE HARD BUT NOT NEARLY AS DIFFICULT AS SPENDING OUR LIVES RUNNING FROM IT. EMBRACING OUR VULNERABILITIES IS RISKY BUT NOT NEARLY AS DANGEROUS AS GIVING UP ON LOVE AND BELONGING AND JOY — THE EXPERIENCES THAT MAKE US THE MOST VULNERABLE. ONLY WHEN WE ARE BRAVE ENOUGH TO EXPLORE THE DARKNESS WILL WE DISCOVER THE INFINITE POWER OF OUR LIGHT." **BRENÉ BROWN**

financially f*cked vs resilient vs well

I've been described many times by people who know me well as resilient. That's because those few people who know my personal background, who understand what I've come through, who have an insight into what I've survived, know that most of these experiences are undetectable to most people.

Professionally, I've also been called resilient. That's because I'm able to push through, to rally for Plan B, C, D, to see what others can't and to take the next step that someone else won't.

I know that being described as resilient is meant as a compliment – and I accept that. After all, the definition of resilience is the capacity to recover quickly from difficulties.

However, that's not all I want for myself. Or all I want for you.

Think back to the question I asked you in the first chapter of this book. If I asked you, 'do you want to be financially resilient or do you want to have financial wellness?', I hope that by now you'd answer with a resounding, 'FINANCIAL WELLNESS'.

I want you to aim for resilience if you need it for where you're at today. But, ultimately, I want you to set your sights higher.

That's because I don't ever want resilience to be our end game.

When it comes to our finances we're often told to be resilient. Which is a good thing, because ultimately we want to be able to weather storms.

But is simply weathering storms truly living?

Which is why I believe, when it comes to our finances, our businesses (and let's be honest, all of our lives) we should be aiming for wellness.

To not simply grit our teeth and bear our financial situation, or wait for Prince Charming, a fairy godmother or a fantasy lotto ticket to come rescue us – but, instead, to become the author of our own financial story.

A story you're actually excited about.

One that not only protects you, but allows you to live out your goals and aspirations.

If you're a business owner I want this financial wellness to spill over to your business. I want you to resolve to sit down and look at the numbers regularly, but embrace all parts of business ownership knowing that when you do, you'll not only weather the storms, but also enjoy the sunshine.

Now, I've been a long-time advocate of financial wellness and, hopefully, after reading this book you are too.

Perhaps you picked up this book knowing you needed to unf*ck your finances. What I hope you've realised is that you are capable of so much more than that.

My hope is that you're already moving through the stages of becoming financially unf*cked, to financially resilient to financially well. You're excited about designing the life you love and you have a sneaky suspicion you can actually do it.

Guess what? I know you can!

But don't keep me in the dark. Go do it. Financially adult, financially stuff up, financially dust yourself off and try again. Move from being financially f*cked, to financially resilient to financially well.

And absolutely let me know how you're going.

I can't wait to hear your real-life financial fairy tales.

apps and solutions we love

"LIFE ISN'T ABOUT FINDING YOURSELF.
LIFE IS ABOUT CREATING YOURSELF."
GEORGE BERNARD SHAW

SPENDING & TRACKING APPS

Money Dashboard (free)

Money Hub (paid)

Yolt (free)

Pocketbook (free)

Chip (free)

OTHER COOL APPS

Acorns (free to download, but monthly fee)

Splitwise (free)

ATM Hunter (free)

TOOLS AND RESOURCES

Head to the Unf*ck Your Finances blog at themoneybarre.com.au and download the many tools and exercises mentioned in this book.

COURSES

The Unf*ck Your Finances online courses: www.unfckyourfinances.com

OTHER SITES YOU MIGHT WANT TO CHECK OUT OR I'VE MENTIONED IN THE BOOK

Alexx Stuart Low Cost Living

www.lowtoxlife.com

Ted Talk: Simon Sinek: How Great Leaders Inspire Action

Ted Talk: Brené Brown: The Power of Vulnerability

Open Shed (sharing website)

moneyadviceservice.org.uk

COMPARISON SITES

GoCompare.com

MoneySuperMarket.com

ComparetheMarket.com

RECOMMENDED READING

Mastering the Money Game, Tony Robbins

Good to Great, Jim Collins

On Purpose, Karen James

Richest Man in Babylon, George S. Clason

Rich Dad Poor Dad, Robert Kiyosaki

Spent, Dr Frank Lipman

More Money for Shoes, Melissa Browne

Fabulous but Broke, Melissa Browne

about Mel

Melissa Browne (Mel) is an author and serial entrepreneur. She is CEO of the award-winning accounting and advisory firm A&TA (Accounting & Taxation Advantage), CEO of the Financial Planning Business For 28–48-Year-Olds who want to financially grow up, The Money Barre, and Director of Business at the long-day early learning school for 3–5-year-olds, Thinkers.inq. Three very different businesses, but all are pushing the boundaries in their fields, questioning what is possible and disrupting their industry in order to create the best possible results for their communities.

Mel also uses her unique, sometimes irreverent but always inspiring voice to speak and write about all things numbers, business, money, entrepreneurship and strategy. Her first book is the illustrated business book, *More Money for Shoes*, which compares building a business to building a wardrobe and shows you how to build a profitable, successful business. Her second book, *Fabulous but Broke*, is another illustrated book and uses financial fairy tales to challenge money messages that readers may have and question the notion that you need a fairy godmother or knight in shining armour to save you.

Melissa also writes a fortnightly column for the money section in the *Sydney Morning Herald* and Melbourne's *The Age*, is a regular contributor to *Latte Magazine* and *Gloss Magazine*, and has made regular TV appearances including on the *Today Show*, *Weekend Sunrise*, *Weekend Today*, *Seven News*, *Sky Business* and *The Daily Edition*. She has also been featured in or has written articles for *CEO Magazine, Cosmopolitan, Elle, The Collective, Harpers Bazaar, Ragtrader, Rendezvous* and *Madison*. In 2013 she was featured as one of Australia's 100 most inspiring women in *Madison* magazine and in 2016 was listed as one of Westpac's and the *Financial Review*'s '100 Women of Influence'.

Mel's personal mission is to help women around the world find their voice and become both business and financially savvy. Or to put it simply, she delights in creating transformational change. Moving people from where they are to somewhere that's even better than what they imagined. Mel is driven by her own story and her own experience of resilience to help others understand that it doesn't matter where you're from or what you've been through – you can not just overcome but you can succeed.

Mel is regularly asked to speak to groups and organisations and has been described as an entertaining and thought-provoking speaker who has the ability to make topics that people normally don't care about, interesting and challenging.

And if you're curious about just how many pairs of shoes she owns? She'll never tell.

You can find more about Mel at melissabrowne.com.au

work with us

THE UNF*CK YOUR FINANCES ONLINE COURSES

unfckyourfinances.com

Yes, you've read the book – but if you're honest, you need a little bit more help. That is why we have created more intensive online solutions to help you. Here you'll find modules that dive further into those money chapters and subjects that you find tricky (or even a bit icky). You can buy one at a time or sign up for the whole lot.

THE MONEY BARRE

themoneybarre.com.au

At The Money Barre we're all about helping our members develop financial fitness, strength and flexibility. We want to help you design the life you want as well as helping you develop options for whoever you are and wherever you find yourself in life.

We know that most of us develop a growing awareness when we started working that maybe we should do something about our finances. This is followed by a moment (which hopefully happens before we turn fifty!) that it's time to 'sort ourselves out', financially speaking.

That's your cue to meet us at The Money Barre.

You might want someone to work with you to help you get out of the mess you've found yourself in, understand how best to manage your money, or develop a sophisticated financial strategy for you. You want someone who will understand where you are now, where you want to go, what your values are and who can help you become financially fit and strong so you have the flexibility to adapt to whatever life throws at you.

Whether it's financial coaching through our Mini Barre, sorting your whole mess out, insurance, investment or sorting out your super, we're the no-nonsense trustworthy solution you've been looking for. Designed for Gens X and Y.

First published by King Street Press.

This edition first published in Great Britain in 2018 by Trapeze,
an imprint of The Orion Publishing Group Ltd
Carmelite House, 50 Victoria Embankment,
London EC4Y 0DZ

An Hachette UK company

10 9 8 7 6 5 4 3 2 1

A CIP catalogue record for this book is
available from the British Library.

ISBN (trade paperback): 978 1 4091 8717 2
ISBN (ebook): 978 1 4091 8718 9

Printed and bound by CPI Group (UK) Ltd, Croydon, CR0 4YY

www.orionbooks.co.uk